Christianity Lite

Christianity Lite

A PASTOR'S STRUGGLE WITH A HEAVY-HANDED RELIGION

Jimmy R. Watson

RESOURCE *Publications* · Eugene, Oregon

CHRISTIANITY LITE
A Pastor's Struggle with a Heavy-Handed Religion

Copyright © 2025 Jimmy R. Watson. All rights reserved. Except for brief quotations in critical publications or reviews, no part of this book may be reproduced in any manner without prior written permission from the publisher. Write: Permissions, Wipf and Stock Publishers, 199 W. 8th Ave., Suite 3, Eugene, OR 97401.

Resource Publications
An Imprint of Wipf and Stock Publishers
199 W. 8th Ave., Suite 3
Eugene, OR 97401

www.wipfandstock.com

PAPERBACK ISBN: 979-8-3852-5560-3
HARDCOVER ISBN: 979-8-3852-5561-0
EBOOK ISBN: 979-8-3852-5562-7

Unless otherwise marked, Scripture quotations are taken from the New Revised Standard Version Updated Edition. Copyright © 2021 National Council of Churches of Christ in the United States of America. Used by permission. All rights reserved worldwide.
Scripture quotations marked (CEB) from the COMMON ENGLISH BIBLE. © Copyright 2011
COMMON ENGLISH BIBLE. All rights reserved. Used by permission. (www.CommonEnglishBible.com).

I dedicate this book to everyone who thinks it is
ridiculous to rumble over religion
foolish to fight over faith
dumb to dispute doctrine
silly to spar over spirituality
corrosive to cross swords over Christianity.

Contents

Introduction ix

Chapter 1: A Lite Approach to Christianity 1

Chapter 2: God 25

Chapter 3: Jesus 37

Chapter 4: The Holy Spirit 50

Chapter 5: The Bible 60

Chapter 6: Church Vitality 71

Chapter 7: Church Polity 84

Chapter 8: The Gospel 93

Chapter 9: Spirituality 103

Chapter 10: Prayer 112

Chapter 11: Evangelism 119

Chapter 12: Eschatology 127

Chapter 13: Sin 132

Chapter 14: Grace 141

Chapter 15: The Heavy Issue of Identity 150

Bibliography 157

Introduction

FROM DAY ONE AS a local church pastor, I have had an uneasy feeling about my profession. What led me into the ministry is a long, convoluted story that is probably not suitable for readers who need their pastors to have a clearly articulated "calling". Nevertheless, in January 1990 I planted my feet in a pulpit that I would occupy for the next few years, followed by numerous other pulpits I have settled into in the last three-and-a-half decades.

Until recently, I have been unable to put my finger on the origin of my uneasiness. There are times when I convince myself that I am suffering from a chronic case of imposter syndrome. As I reflect on what that means, I tend to think that either we pastors are *all* imposters or none of us are. Pastors are people, mere mortals, so unless one is suffering from a severe case of narcissism there must be a constant drumbeat of doubt concerning the authenticity and sincerity of one's calling.

I have dabbled with other possible reasons for my uneasiness or low-level anxiety, such as the jealousy I have harbored about the success or income of people who have chosen other professions. "I could have done better," I tell myself as I listen to some of my parishioners share their adventurous life stories with me. However, perhaps this is the best thing I could have ever chosen for myself. As a friend and parishioner once said to me, "Jimmy, being a pastor is the most radical thing you could have ever done." True or not, I will carry this mystery to my grave.

Looking back, I do believe I accidentally stumbled upon an explanation for my uneasiness in an early conversation I had with a relative who asked me, incredulously, why I had chosen the path of ministry. Without thinking I blurted out the words, "To help people become *less religious.*" Both of us probably assumed I was being sarcastic, if not disingenuous. Surely, I didn't believe that did I? Isn't that like saying I became a teacher to

Introduction

help people become less educated or a soldier to make the world less safe? What exactly does "less religious" even mean?

I tried to put that episode out of my mind, but it never left. It lingers like a jalapeno burn on the lips. I have never quite come to terms with saying something so seemingly counterintuitive. At the same time, I *have* come to terms with the possibility that my thoughtless utterance was instinctively true for me then and now, that I do want people to be *less religious*, but didn't know how to articulate that until I scanned my Facebook page one ordinary day in the late summer of 2023. In the blink of an eye, the intellectual grounding of my decades-long religious instincts began to take shape.

On August 29, 2023, *The New York Times* published an interview with the prominent American atheist, Daniel Dennett. The journalist, David Marchese, asked the recently deceased Dennett about his sister, a clergyperson in my denomination, the United Church of Christ.[1] Dennett responded,

> My older sister is the white sheep of the family. She went to seminary and was ordained late in her life. She's still alive. She was raised in the Congregational Church, which became part of what's now the United Church of Christ, which is *religion lite*. If all religion were like that, all religion would be fantastic.[2]

When this article came out, my UCC colleagues and friends went bananas. They didn't know whether to be offended or flattered. Obviously, when Dennett referred to us as "religion lite," he meant it as a complement, although he didn't elaborate on what he meant by either "religion lite" or "fantastic." As I reflected on his terse critique of us, I began to think that maybe he was on to something. Maybe we *are* religion lite, sort of like lite beer or sugar-free candy, which doesn't seem bad to me.

As I reflected on Dennett's words, I began to sense that he was expressing what I had tried to articulate decades ago to my curious cousin. What I termed "less religious," Dennett clarifies as "religion lite," and yet I still needed to explore what this means. This book, therefore, is my attempt to connect "religion lite" to my faith tradition, Christianity. I have always suspected that my brand of Christianity is a *moderate* expression of religion within the context of Christian history, in contrast to expressions

---

1. Daniel Clement Dennett III, passed away on April 19, 2024.
2. Marchese, "How to Live a Happy Life."

Introduction

of Christianity that are much more heavy-handed, insensitive, oppressive, narrow-minded, and overbearing.

Heavy-handed Christianity believes it has the upper hand in terms of faithfulness to God. It claims to occupy the moral and spiritual high ground, and yet I have always been uncomfortable around folks who are laboriously religious, people who define themselves as devout, pious, reverent, godly, pure, and God-fearing. The flavor of heavy-handed religion is saturated with such things as certainty, assurance (blessed or not!), authority, conviction, inflexibility, and extremism. In terms of how accessible it is to folks, it is complex, complicated, confusing, and convoluted. In terms of its practicality, it is unfeasible, unworkable, and largely unattainable, creating undue anxiety, worry, and distress. Some adherents to a weightier expression of religion have escaped with the lingering scars of PTSD. What is sorely needed in our society (and others) is a moderate expression of religion, what I have labeled "Christianity Lite."

Not everyone agrees with my critique of religion in this manner. A quick internet search for "Christianity Lite" unearths several recent videos and articles that are critical of what they consider to be just a watered-down version of Christianity. One YouTube video produced by the satirical Christian site, *The Babylon Bee*, portrays a group of young people as undisciplined, gay-friendly, smoking and drinking couch surfers, supported by Satan, who have "no guilt and judgment." A Christianity Lite meme posted on Reddit is a picture of an iceberg—small on the surface, massive under the surface. The caption above reads "Western European Christianity," while the iceberg below the surface is labeled "Unchanged pagan rituals and superstitions," as if Christianity Lite is a contemporary manifestation of paganism (whatever that is). In essence, critics think of Christianity Lite as something less faithful than "true" Christianity.

I am using the term "Christianity Lite" in a different way than is expressed on these internet sites. I am using it in a way that expresses a faith that is less heavy-handed than traditional Christianity, and yet, in my view, potentially more faithful, sincere, and authentic. The word "lite," as expressed in this book, is similar to what is used in relation to low-fat, low-sugar, or low-caloric versions of food and drink products, such as "Miller Lite." Specifically, the word denotes "an innocuous or unthreatening version" of the Christian faith.[3] I am suggesting that a preferable presentation

---

3. "Lite," Merriam-Webster (adjective), http://www.merriam-webster.com.

Introduction

of Christianity and/or religion in general should be less complicated and overwhelming than what we have inherited.

All throughout this book, I will distinguish between Christianity Lite and a heavy-handed Christianity while making the case that the former is worthier of our consideration than the latter. Maybe it's time to lighten up, to lighten the mood, to be more light-hearted, to promote a religious version of a smaller carbon footprint—"religion lite" as Dennett calls it. Because of my largely Christian (or Christian adjacent) audience, I will narrow down Dennett's concept to *Christianity* Lite and share my impressions of what that might be.

The essays in this book are a sampling of what a moderate expression of Christianity might look and feel like. I have divided the book into fifteen chapters, each with multiple essays. In chapter 1, I offer a wide range of possible characteristics of Christianity (and Religion) Lite, using words such as emptiness, decluttering, uncertainty, simplicity, do-ability, efficiency, and hybridity. In the next four chapters, I present a moderate expression of God, Jesus, the Holy Spirit, and the Bible. In chapters 6-7, I explore issues related to church viability and polity. In the next seven chapters, I examine what Christianity Lite might look like in terms of the gospel, spirituality, prayer, evangelism, eschatology, sin, and grace. In chapter 15, I will conclude with a lite look at identity issues within the Christian tradition.

In addition to my attempt to define and clarify "Christianity Lite," this book illustrates a lite expression of the faith with essays featuring creative, playful, imaginative analogies. In no way does this book cover all the bases of Christianity Lite. It barely gets us to first base, and yet it can serve as a guide for the moderately religious to contemplate and practice their faith in ways that do not destroy credibility.

1

A Lite Approach to Christianity

RUNNING ON EMPTY

A YEAR AFTER I earned my driver's license, the American singer-songwriter, Jackson Browne, recorded the song *Running on Empty*. He wrote the song while driving to the studio each day to record music for his previous album. According to *Rolling Stone* magazine, Browne said, "I was always driving around with no gas in the car. I just never bothered to fill up the tank because—how far was it anyway? Just a few blocks."[1] Being just a few blocks away from our destination is usually not the case when we're running on empty. Imagine that you're driving down the interstate and the low fuel light comes on. You see a gas station up ahead but decide to wait until the next one comes along. After a while you become aware that you have neglected to keep an eye out for a gas station, and now, with none in sight, you see that your fuel is getting dangerously low. Running on fumes low. You say to yourself, "What was I thinking when I passed the last couple of gas stations? I guess I was distracted."

But now you're *not* distracted. You are much more attuned to your driving. Your eyes are not wandering from side to side checking out the scenery off the highway. You are more attentive to how fast you are going, knowing that going slower saves gas, and yet at the same time you are in a hurry to get to the nearest gas station, wherever that is. You know that if you get distracted again you might miss the next exit and completely run

---

1. Nelson, "Jackson Browne."

out of gas, so you stay laser-focused on what you are doing. Then it dawns on you: *You are a better driver while running on empty.*

Likewise, we are more attuned to our spiritual, mental, emotional, and physical well-being when we feel like we are running on empty, when we feel like we are running on fumes, when we feel like we're a little light in the tank. When this happens, we are riding shotgun with the Spirit.

The Apostle Paul, in the second chapter of his letter to the Philippians, presents a lite picture of a Jesus who is running on empty. Paul tells the Philippians to learn from Jesus' example and become less full of themselves, to "regard others as better than" us, to focus on the interests of others rather than our own interests. According to Paul, Jesus thought that a full tank of divinity is something only for God. He (Jesus) "did not regard equality with God (a full tank) as something to be grasped, but emptied himself." In this cosmic, pre-incarnate, before-birth-in-a-Bethlehem-barn Christology, Jesus began with a full tank of divinity but then punches a hole in the gas tank and lets it run dry. At that point, we are gifted with the incarnation. Jesus is presented in human form—the "form of a slave, being born in human likeness." Paul refers to this as an act of humility.

Can you think of anything more humbling, if not humiliating, than draining the divine tank to become human? And what is the most humiliating thing that could happen to a human being? Slipping on a banana peel? Walking out of a restroom with toilet paper stuck to our shoes? Nope. *Death by public execution* is the most humiliating thing that can happen to a human being, especially an innocent human being. Paul writes, "He (Jesus) humbled himself and became obedient to the point of death—even death on a cross"—the Empire's preferred method of public execution. While Jesus is dying on the cross, he cries out, "My God, my God, why have you forsaken me?"[2] This is the moment Jesus realizes his tank is empty, symbolized poignantly by the soldier piercing his side to make sure everything has been drained out.[3]

The conclusion of the Jesus story is a two-act play: humiliation (death) and exaltation (resurrection). A God tank that has been self-emptied, siphoned away like a thief in the night, becomes a tank that is eternally full of divinity. And divine gas gets good gas mileage. Paul continues: "Therefore God exalted him even more highly (filled his tank all the way up) and gave him the name that is above every other name"—a Premium name,

---

2. Mt. 27:46.

3. Jn. 19:34.

to use gas pump lingo, so that the humility of being human is no longer humiliating—"so that at the name given to Jesus," his human name, every knee—every creaking, popping, arthritic, sore, stiff, or flexible knee should bend, "in heaven and on earth and under the earth, and every tongue"—every stammering, stuttering, or smooth-talking tongue, language, dialect, or accent should confess that Jesus of Nazareth, the Christ or Messiah, "is Lord to the glory of God the Father." The tank is now full. Very full. Paul is claiming that Jesus' emptiness—his lite-ness—prepares him for his exaltation or fullness. He empties his tank of Regular Unleaded so that he can fill it with Premium Unleaded.

Aside from all the questionable, debatable, hyperbolic, and potentially problematic Christology here, what does this mean for you and me? It means that we drive better, spiritually speaking, if we feel like we are running on empty. It means we should practice spiritual humility and be careful being "too full of ourselves." *That* is Christianity Lite.

Some of us have spent time in Pentecostal or charismatic settings, as I did back in the early 1980s. In that setting, I remember people claiming they were "*filled* with the Spirit" or "Spirit-*filled*." I don't doubt the sincerity and passion of people who use that terminology—I used it myself. However, to claim that one is Spirit-filled is to claim that we contain God—we are *God's* tanks! Isn't it more theologically accurate to say that God contains us? "*In God* we live and move and have our being,"[4] Paul tells the Athenians. Nowhere does he say, "*In us* God lives and moves and has God's being." It is more accurate to say that God is "human-filled, creation-filled, world-filled" than to say that we are "Spirit-filled." God is *our* tank; we are not God's tank.

To claim that one is Spirit-filled implies that we have a full tank of divinity, something even Jesus denied for himself when he was found in "human likeness." If Jesus wasn't Spirit-filled, if he ran on empty all the way to the cross, then I don't see how we can claim with a straight face to be Spirit-filled. When someone says they are Spirit-filled the implication is that others are not. This is an extremely "full of themselves" assumption. Personally, when I realized the arrogance of thinking this way, I siphoned out all the gas in my God tank and started over, which is how I ended up in the United Church of Christ, a church that a prominent atheist refers to as "Religion Lite."

---

4. Acts 17:28 (italics mine).

Christianity Lite

THE ART OF DECLUTTERING

A few years ago, Marie Kondo, the Japanese decluttering expert, was getting all the headlines. Her book, *The Life-Changing Magic of Tidying Up: The Japanese Art of Decluttering and Organizing*, took Japan, Europe, and then the United States by storm. There are, and have been, other decluttering experts, but what makes her work so popular is her underlying philosophy about decluttering and tidying up. She makes it more than a chore. She makes it interesting. A *New York Times* article referred to her approach to decluttering as "somewhat radical and spiritual." She has two main themes for her decluttering philosophy. First, discard everything that does not "spark joy." Thank the objects that are getting the heave-ho for their service and then let them go. Second, do not buy any more organizing equipment because your home already has all it needs. If you must buy more boxes, bins, shelves, etc., then you have too much stuff, so go back to point number one.[5]

We can apply Kondo's philosophical approach to decluttering our religious traditions, including, but not limited to our belief systems, religious rituals, spiritual disciplines, moral views, and volunteer work. First, do these things spark joy? If not, then offer thanks to them for their past service and send them packing. Years ago, I volunteered for a couple of summers at a church camp. Overall, because of heavy-handed camp leadership, it was a terrible experience. It boiled over the second summer when I helped a group of high school kids create a communion service based on the Creation story from the book of Genesis. It featured kids dressed up like Adam and Eve and animals and trees, all taking part at the "Open table" of Christ. Ironically, the camp director didn't appreciate creativity applied to the Creation story. I received a formal complaint from the camp. This experience did not spark joy, so after that summer I never volunteered at that camp again.

We should say "thank you" to those things that may have served us well in the past but no longer bring us joy. Things that have become, to use the Apostle Paul's word, *rubbish*. Lose the religious rubbish. Toss it out. Get rid of it, take it to Goodwill, have a yard sale, rummage sale, or an auction, or just put it in a trash bin and make sure you get it to the curb before the garbage truck comes by. The Apostle Paul likely never enjoyed

---

5. "Marie Kondo and the Life-Changing Magic of Japanese Soft Power," January 18, 2019.

the convenience of trash pickup day, but he knew all about religious decluttering. He writes, "For his (Jesus') sake I have suffered the *loss* of all things, and I regard them as rubbish, in order that I may gain Christ."[6] Paul is into some serious spiritual decluttering here. He doesn't just rummage through his religion and throw out a *few* things, he throws out *everything*. That's not necessary for me and you, but Paul has a lot more things to chunk. Specifically, he must get rid of the confidence he has in his religious pedigree. He isn't getting rid of his pedigree—you can't do that. He is getting rid of the confidence he has in his pedigree to secure his place in God's realm.

His pedigree couldn't have been more impressive. Paul was a circumcised Israelite from the respected tribe of Benjamin— "a Hebrew born of Hebrews"—a Pharisee, a zealous persecutor of a heretical sect of messianic Jews (Christians), and he claimed to be a righteous follower of the Law. He had it all.[7] A similarly pedigreed person today would be surrounded by bodyguards and an entourage. One day Paul and his entourage encounter the Christ on his way to a "persecution party" in Damascus.[8] Dramatically, he converts to the Messianic sect, and it doesn't take long for him to conclude that his padded pedigree no longer sparks joy in his life. It no longer sparks confidence, so he humorously refers to it as *skubalon* or "rubbish."[9]

I surveyed all the major English translations of the Bible and learned that *skubalon* is variously translated as rubbish, garbage, nothing, dung, dog dung, refuse, dirt, dregs, sewer trash, worthless trash, worthless, filth, excrement, pile of waste, and my favorite translation: drit and turds. I kid you not. Drit refers to bird feces. I probably don't need to tell you what the actual "R" rated translation of *skubalon* is. If Paul had grown up in my parent's generation, his momma might have washed his mouth out with soap. Nevertheless, what we can glean from Paul is that there are things in our religious traditions and institutions that do not bring us across the threshold of God's realm. They do not spark joy; therefore, they need to be chunked, tossed out the window, discarded, or thrown away. Sometimes we just need to lighten our religion with good old-fashioned decluttering.

---

6. Phil. 3:8.
7. Phil. 3:5–6.
8. Acts 9:3–8.
9. "skubalon," Bible Hub, "rubbish" (noun), http://www.biblehub.com.

WHATEVER RELIGION

Whatever Religion is religion with a light touch. It is open-wide and open-ended, spacious and gracious, flexible and forgiving, elastic and fantastic, welcoming and *whatever*. Whatever Religion contrasts with *What Is* Religion. What Is Religion is inflexible, set in stone, black and white, heavy-handed religion. *Whatever* Religion, on the other hand, allows room to grow. When parents go school shopping for their small children, sometimes they buy clothes that are a size larger than they need because they know the child will soon grow into them. We should approach religion and spirituality this way. It should be loose and baggy because we need room to grow. Whatever Religion also needs us to be light on our feet—Fred Astaire-like faith. It requires us to be nimble because we don't know where this dance is going to take us.

The Hebrew Scriptures offer hints of a Whatever *God*. In the story from Exodus 32, Moses and his people are in their post-slavery Wilderness Wandering days. He has climbed Mt. Sinai to retrieve the Ten Commandments (which is literally religion set in stone—Moses doesn't yet "get it"). Apparently chiseling a Top Ten list on stone tablets is a time-consuming event. The people get antsy waiting for their fearless leader to come down from the mountain. They need some blessed assurance that they are keeping things kosher, so to speak. They believe they need a What Is Religion, so they go to Moses' brother, Aaron, and ask that he "make gods" for them, solid gods one can touch and hold, what we call idols.

Now, it's not what you think. They aren't trying to be unfaithful to God; they don't even *know* God at this point. They ask Aaron to make "gods," plural. This is a time in history when monotheism, the belief in only one God, has not yet captured the imagination of the people. In their Egyptian days, they were exposed to polytheistic religion, the belief in many gods. They must have thought, "Let's just go with that. Aaron, please do us a solid and make some, er, gods for us. We will supply whatever you need." They are even willing to let loose their gold to make it so. What benefits are precious metals in the desert anyway? So, Aaron takes their gold and makes an image of a calf because the calf or young bull was a common image for certain Canaanite gods. This makes sense because they are heading toward the land of Canaan. Surely, these are the gods that await them.

We can't blame them for their error in judgment. After all, Moses had only recently met the One True God in a burning bush (not exactly something one can touch and hold), and when Moses asks for a name, God gives a Whatever response: "I am."[10] (Try that the next time someone asks you for your name.) A golden image of a calf seems like a good call. Of course, it turns out that no image is appropriate because an idol, a solid image of God, represents a heavy-handed, limited, inflexible What Is God. But "I Am" is a Whatever God, an open-wide and open-ended, spacious and gracious, flexible and forgiving, elastic and fantastic, welcoming God. And who does a Whatever God invite into the kingdom of God? *Whoever*.

Jesus gets it. He is a proponent of Whatever Religion rather than What Is Religion. He is a proponent of religion that offers an open invitation to an open table rather than requiring an RSVP for VIPs. We see this clearly in Jesus' parable of the Marriage Feast.[11] A king gives a banquet for his son. At first, he invites all the *Who's Who* folks, the elites, the movers and the shakers of What Is Religion. But they aren't fond of the king, so they decline in ways that are not very kind to those handing out the invitations. Then the king sends his messengers out into the streets to invite Whoever's rather than Who's Who. The Whoever's all come wearing traditional wedding garments. To show respect to the bride and groom, all the guests are wearing the same type of clothing. No one is outshining anyone else with their fashion sense. No guest can put on airs at this wedding feast.

But one person crashes the party wearing his own clothing, probably a double-vested suit, silk tie and kerchief, gold cufflinks, and Italian leather loafers. He wants to stand out. He knows the other Who's Who folks in the kingdom are not going to be there (most are now dead), so now is his chance to be the big fish in a little pond, to be the big man on campus. But when the king sees that he is not wearing a common wedding gown, he is thrown out of the feast.

This parable is about a Whatever God in a Whoever Kingdom of God. It is about religion with a light touch, open-wide and open-ended, spacious and gracious, flexible and forgiving, elastic and fantastic, welcoming and *whatever*. The only person thrown out is the person who prefers a What Is God in a What Is Kingdom of God.

And then there's the Apostle Paul. He also gets it. Paul is the author of Whatever Religion's Statement of Faith, National Anthem, Pledge of Allegiance, and Constitution all rolled into one: "Whatever is true, whatever is honorable, whatever is just, whatever is pure, whatever is pleasing, whatever is commendable, if there is any excellence and if there is anything

---

10. Ex. 3:14.
11. Mt. 22:1–14.

worthy of praise, think about these things."[12] Notice he doesn't define what any of these are because this is religion without strong-armed coercion. It is undefined on purpose because each generation of Christ-followers needs to determine for themselves what *is* true, honorable, just, pure, pleasing, commendable, excellent, and worthy of praise. This is why we need to wear baggy clothes (metaphorically speaking). We need room to grow in this Whatever Religion, a possibility only in a lite expression of Christianity.

B-SIDE

Back in the day people of a certain age listened to 45's, those little vinyl discs that had an "A-side" and a "B-side". Most of the time, we bought them for the A-side, the song that was predicted to be the hit single. It was the music producer's best shot at selling records and getting a generous amount of radio airplay. The B-side (or "flip side") was a recording that usually received less attention. It was thought to be a filler song of lower quality, and yet the two songs occupying opposing sides of a 45 were in competition with one another. On occasion, the B-side was more of a commercial success than the A-side. We don't see many 45s these days, unless one is browsing through a used music store. That's because in the 1960s the music industry slowly shifted from releasing singles with A and B sides to full album releases. By the time I began purchasing music in the mid-70s, albums were in greater demand than singles.[13]

Competition is the way of the world. It's built into our DNA. "Survival of the Fittest," the driving force behind the theory of evolution, is basically about competition for food and females. That sounds sexist . . . because it is. Competition dominates the headlines from sports' rivals to elections to military conflict. Aside from the headlines, almost everything we do is related to some kind of competition: Fighting for control of the television remote, who's going to do the laundry, games and grades, sports and spelling bees, competing for a mate or mineral rights, luring new customers to your business, billboard signs, sibling rivalries—much of our lives are built upon the slab of competition, the driving force behind our survival as a species.

Competition is also the unspoken driving force behind the survival of religious institutions. Drive around any community in the United States

---

12. Phil 4:8.
13. Garn, "Needle Me This."

and what do you see? Steeples and well-lit or nicely painted church signs on every corner, all representing a different flavor of faith. We might not say this out loud, but we are all competing for the affection of the people. Some congregations will survive long-term, and others will not.

Another unspoken truism is that there is an A-side and a B-side to Christianity. The A-side is the one that gets the most airtime (often literally on television and radio). It is more in tune with our culture and therefore more competitive. It pulls out all the stops. A-side Christianity is more aggressive and heavy-handed in its evangelism methods. If someone knocks on your door to invite you to their church, it's usually a representative from an A-side congregation because they are more confident that they will play the best song, so to speak. Unfortunately, A-side Christianity tends to have more of an us vs. them mentality.

Not long ago, someone outside of my congregation said to me over breakfast, "Pastor, do you think we're losing?" I could tell he was talking as a culture warrior. Because I didn't want to disagree with him overtly, which might have led to an early morning under-caffeinated argument, I decided to give a coy response: "Who are we competing against?" My question sounded foreign to him because in his mind Christianity is out to *win*. Winning souls is the primary goal of a non-Lite Christianity.

On the flipside, B-side Christianity is overall less competitive, less popular, less known, less aggressive, and unfortunately less confident. It doesn't get as much airtime. And yet, I believe the B-side plays a better song these days. B-side Christianity is less competitive by nature, but that hasn't always been the case. Pardon the phonographic pun, but the turn tables have turned. In the mid-twentieth century, mainline Protestantism *was* the A-side of Christianity. It was very popular, and it had almost all the airtime on television, radio, newspapers and magazines. Beginning in the 1970s, however, mainline Protestantism became *sideline* Protestantism. It is now the B-side. These days we're like a record with a scratch on it. Few people want to listen to us. We are less popular and get less airtime than we used to, and yet I still believe we can produce good music.

The competition between A-side and B-side religion has been around since the time Moses saw the B-side, or rather the backside, of God. In Exodus 33, Moses has a little chat with God and expresses his desire for God to be fully present with him and the Israelites as they make their way to the land of Canaan. Moses claims that the Israelites are distinct from other peoples, so God should show them favor. "Show us your glory, God, because we are *special*. We are the A-side of humanity." By now, God is getting a little weary of Moses' competitive spirit, so God says to Moses, "Look, what you fail to understand is that I will show grace and mercy to whoever I want. There's nothing special about you or your people. I'm not even going to show you my face, Moses, because you're not ready for that. That much glory and light and truth would probably do you in. But yes, I do fancy you. I like your spunk and persistence, and I appreciate the fact that you left behind your little shepherding business to make a dangerous journey into Egypt to help the Israelites escape slavery. So, here's what I'll do for you. I will wedge your body into the crevice of a rock and when I walk by, I will cover your eyes with my hand, and then after I am well past you, I will remove my hand and then you will see my backside." As God passes by, I can just hear Moses say, "Hey God, I've got your back."

This is the day God taught Moses that "backside" or B-side religion is, or can be, a good song because it's *not* as competitive. It doesn't lay it on thick claiming the love of God is for its followers only. It doesn't declare that its followers are the only ones who have seen God face-to-face or heard God's voice. It doesn't allege that its followers are distinct from other people or persuasions, much less superior. It doesn't brag about having all the truth and light of God. It doesn't declare that it alone is a recipient of God's grace. It doesn't insist that God has reserved God's mercy for its followers. It doesn't gloat about God's glory. It doesn't boast, crow, talk big, blow its own trumpet, toot its own horn, or sing its own praises. It doesn't compete using combative congregants and their cutthroat creeds, dog-eat-dog doctrines, and ruthless rules. Christianity Lite is B-side religion, and the music is damn good.

LESS IS MORE

Christianity Lite is like Bud Light without the alcohol content or social conflict.[14] It has fewer calories than traditional dominant expressions of religion, but it still tastes good. And just as a diet can be good for you, so can Christianity Lite. It is preferable to religion that is heavy-handed, especially for folks who have had harmful experiences in the church. At the very least, religion with a lighter touch is not the sort of religion that burns

---

14. The Bud Light controversy began with a promotional partnership featuring transgender influencer Dylan Mulvaney, which sparked a conservative backlash and calls for a boycott.

people on the stake (literally or figuratively). It allows people more freedom to pursue their own path, search their own souls, and journey with Jesus on their own terms.

Christianity Lite is less religious, which is exactly what I have intuited all these years. But is that a good thing? I think it is because . . . *less is more*. This phrase originated in a 19th century poem by Robert Browning, although it is often associated with the famous architect and furniture designer Ludwig Mies Van Der Rohe (1886–1969). Van Der Rohe was a minimalist. He referred to his buildings as "skin and bones." Minimalism is characterized by simplicity, and he believed wholeheartedly that simplicity is solid, that *less is more*. That which is not overly designed is visually appealing. Interior designers and decorators will tell you that cluttered spaces are less attractive than rooms with more empty space.

Similarly, when something is verbally understated, it can be more powerful and effective than if it is flashy and flamboyant. "Less is more" applies to the speaking professions or just telling a story to our friends. Fewer details make the story easier to grasp.

"Less is more" seems contradictory because the words *less* and *more* are antonyms: They are one another's literal opposite. And yet, it is a tried-and-true principle, even in terms of our religious faith. Jesus's response to the lawyer in Matthew 22:34–46 is a classic example. The lawyer asks Jesus, "Teacher, which commandment in the law is the greatest?" To the average person in that time and place that would have been more difficult than a Final Jeopardy answer . . . or is it a question? The lawyer was referring to the 613 commandments in the Hebrew Scriptures, collectively called the mitzvoth. Many of these commandments were extremely heavy-handed and burdensome. In fact, the word "commandment" itself is a heavy-handed word. Mitzvoth is *not* an example of Religion Lite. Here are just a few examples of some of the hard-to-follow commandments found in the mitzvoth:

- There is a commandment to destroy a city that has turned into idol worship.
- There is a commandment to marry a childless brother's widow.
- There is a commandment not to cut your hair at the temples.[15]

---

15. I don't know about you, but I prefer to have the freedom to make my own hair style choices, even if they're wrong, but at least Elvis was legal in a mitzvoth sense.

Most of the 613 commandments in the mitzvoth do not easily apply to our situation. For its time and place, the mitzvoth might have had some civilizing qualities, but today these commandments sound impractical and silly, if not dangerous and immoral.

The lawyer asks Jesus which of these 613 commandments is the greatest and Jesus, quoting Deuteronomy 6:4, gives a "less is more" answer: "You shall love the Lord your God with all your heart, and with all your soul, and with all your mind." And then, probably because he knew that loving God only matters if we love one another, he includes the commandment from Leviticus 19:18: "You shall love your neighbor as yourself." With that answer to the lawyer's question, Jesus becomes one of the greatest theological minimalists of all time, a proponent and practitioner of Religion Lite. Jesus funnels all his tradition's commandments into two practical commandments. If we can just focus on loving God and neighbor, then everything else is secondary, superfluous, and supercilious. Less is more in the sense of being doable. To use a food analogy, it's better to consume less food that one can chew more thoroughly than to consume excessive amounts of food that cannot be thoroughly chewed. This is what less is more means in terms of our faith. Fewer commandments to chew on equals more people finding a seat at God's dinner table . . . and less choking and puking.

One of the unintended consequences of the mitzvoth is that only those who had the privilege and time to study the law to the extent of that lawyer could possibly claim to follow the law in its entirety and thus be a person in good standing with God. Jesus is having none of that, and yet he isn't "dumbing down" the law; he is "gracing up" the law so that more people can enter the Kingdom of God. Less frivolous or lighter commandments translate into more love, more grace, more mercy, more forgiveness, more peace, more joy, more kindness, more compassion, more faith, more . . . people. This is Christianity Lite. It's less filling, but it tastes great.

THE STATE OF UNCERTAINTY

I have lived most of my life in the state of Texas, yet I have lived *all* my life in a State of Uncertainty. Regardless of whether my physical address is where I pay my taxes, a State of Uncertainty has been where I have received my spiritual mail. My spiritual address has probably changed more often than my physical address, and yet I claim to live in a State of Uncertainty *because*

I am a person of faith.[16] That might sound contradictory, but it's not. If one is a person of faith, they are, by definition, living in a State of Uncertainty. Faith doesn't and cannot live in a State of Certainty, at least not for very long. That's for people who think they have it all figured out. God bless 'em, but that's not faith; that's fundamentalism, which is a very heavy-handed expression of faith.

If a person of sincere, if not authentic, faith—let's call it "Faith Lite"— attempts to migrate to a State of Certainty, the Border Patrol will turn them away if they catch them. People of non-fundamentalist faith seem to have a language all their own and officials in a State of Certainty do not want to be forced to hire bilingual employees. If a person of faith tries to cross into a State of Certainty, they should consider just passing through, although out of curiosity they might linger for a while. At worst, they will find themselves homeless in a State of Certainty. At best, they will resort to couch-surfing, constantly changing their place of residence so they won't be caught. Either way, they don't belong there. Faith doesn't belong anywhere in a permanent sense. If it had a permanent, stagnant, stationary, never-changing address, it wouldn't be faith. Therefore, a person of faith should always carry around a change of address card and have a suitcase packed lightly and ready to go because faith lives on the frontier of spirituality. People of a lite-on-their-feet faith are pioneers, pilgrims, and explorers who live and move and have their being in uncharted territory.

KEEP IT SIMPLE, STUPID

The more complicated our theology is, the less true and accessible it is. I realize this might sound anti-intellectual. Perhaps the reader is thinking that since I am not an academician, I just don't have the intellectual chops to write an informed book about theology.[17] The reader might be right about that to some degree. Even so, that doesn't nullify my comment above. As someone who has stood in the pulpit for well over three decades, trying to interpret and communicate my religious tradition to those who want to be able to understand what I'm saying so they can meditate upon it during the week, I have concluded that the key is to find a balance between too much

---

16. Physically, I have lived in four states and numerous cities, towns, and rural homes, all due to my educational and professional journey.

17. I confess to having a PhD in theology and ethics from Baylor University (1996). I hope that carries, at the very least, some "lite weight."

information and too little information, keeping it simple without resorting to lazy and unnecessary levels of stupidity. Underneath my comment is an even finer theological point, that while absolute truth about divinity is not attainable, relative truth is within our grasp, yet it must be communicated in a way that is within reach of the human brain and connects with the experiences of our species.

Throughout this book, I am utilizing personal opinions, thoughtful theories, and, of course, scripture. On further reflection, I might (unknowingly at times) grab on to one of the four legs of the Wesleyan Quadrilateral: scripture (chiefly, as they say), tradition, reason, and Christian experience. My reliance on this method of theological reflection will at times feel as flexible (and perhaps as dangerous) as a folding chair on an Alabama boat dock.[18]

One of the premises of this book is that the church universal has created a monster. We bear little similarity to the movement Jesus began in that little backwater country in the early first century. We are not able to bear much resemblance, unless we want to undergo a modern equivalent of a crucifixion. If Jesus had an account on a social media platform today, he would have to offer the following disclaimer: "The words and opinions on this page are solely mine, and do not represent the views of the Church that I ostensibly began about two thousand years ago." With that said, however, I do think there is something we can do to align ourselves with Jesus more closely: We can *keep it simple*.

"Keep it simple," along with its cousins, "cut to the chase," "get down to brass tacks," and "get to the point," have always been particles in the air religion breathes. Unfortunately, the smog of complexity, complication, and convolution have hovered over us—the Judeo-Christian tradition—since Day One. And what happens when the air is thick with smoke and pollution? Other than making it difficult to breathe, we become aimless and vulnerable to those whose motives are less pure than the polluted air around us, whose shameful, greedy, and corrupt schemes befoul the currents of Christ. The church has missed the boat in numerous ways, and now we are all trying to swim in dirty water, surrounded by sharks, while flailing our arms in failing flotation devices as we sink under the weighty burden of heavy-handed Christianity.

---

18. "Montgomery Riverfront Brawl," https://en.wikipedia.org.

A Lite Approach to Christianity

DO-ABILITY

Christianity Lite is not just marked by a sense of uncertainty and simplicity; it is also doable. It has its origins in an ancient "to do" list brought forth from the mountain of God. Personally, I would have settled for an emerging prophet stepping into our holy spaces and knocking over furniture, without physically hurting anyone, of course. The story of Jesus causing a shit storm in the Temple is an obvious example of someone trying to help his faith become more doable. Unfortunately, they likely killed him for running off customers that day, so there must be a better way.

The story of Moses climbing down a mountain with a "to do" list is an example of someone trying to make a burgeoning religion more doable. Despite the Israelites' desire to solidify their polytheistic idolization of a Canaanite god in the form of a golden calf, Moses delivers to them what might have been one of history's first "honey-do" lists: The Ten Commandments. None of the commandments carry an unnecessary degree of difficulty. *Do-ability* is implicit in this list designed for Wilderness Wandering people on-the-go. In contemporary terms, here are the Ten Commandments:

1. One God is easier to keep up with than multiple gods.
2. So don't even think about making little statues of other gods. (Oops!)
3. Don't refer to God's name and authority unless you are damn sure God said it, you believe, and that settles it.
4. Find a day to rest so you won't die from exhaustion and blame God.
5. Don't leave your parents behind (if they can keep up with the group).
6. Don't kill anyone because there's no time for a trial and no place for a prison. If you kill someone, we'll just have to kill you Johnny-on-the-spot.
7. Same with dilly-dallying with someone else's spouse.
8. Same with taking other people's stuff.
9. Same with lying about other people.

And don't even act like you want to take someone else's stuff.

According to the Hebrew tradition, Moses receives hundreds of other laws called, not without coincidence, "Mosaic Laws." All of that was fine and good. Centuries later, when these laws were codified by priests who wanted to keep people in line, Israel was well on its way to becoming a strong and viable nation. Until that happened, however, the community of Moses just needed to keep it all simple and doable.

Not much has changed. Today, we are in the same boat, one that is in danger of capsizing if we don't figure out a way to stop from overwhelming the adherents of our potentially beautiful religious tradition with a heavier version of Christianity that likely will capsize our ship. Through the centuries, the church has become a depository of TMI—too much information. Most of it is irrelevant, unnecessary, and maybe (probably) even wrong. We can't unlearn everything that has been thrown our way, but if we want to keep this boat afloat for centuries more (unless climate change, nuclear war, wayward meteors, maniacal Martians, or Donald Trump destroys the world first), then we need to keep Christianity as lite and doable as possible.

DIGGING AND DIGESTING

Traditional Christianity may have already dug itself into too deep a hole. It has evolved into a massive storefront with even larger expanding warehouses of superfluous theological systems and semi-valid assertions. We have made our faith tradition into more than it needs to be. "The more the merrier" philosophy of contemporary Western culture needs to take a backseat to the wisdom of "less is more." There are layers upon layers of varying and often contradictory beliefs, practices, and denominational distinctions. The average person has no choice but to throw their hands up in the air, utter a mild profanity, and either stay home on Sunday mornings, roll the dice and bet on something unfamiliar, or attend the church they are accustomed to.

Another solution is to enroll at a university and pursue a PhD in religious studies so that one can make a more informed choice. However, in terms of the popular anti-elitist interpretation of a "PhD"— "post hole digger"—one would likely use their newly acquired theological education to dig a deeper hole and become even more disconnected from the religious tradition of one's heritage and birth. *Deconstruction* of one's faith and personal theology is all but guaranteed at an institution of higher learning—one that is worth its salt, anyway—which suggests that the metaphorical pole, representing stability and planted-ness, is never actually placed in the hole. If it is, there isn't enough concrete to keep it in there.

It is silly to think we can go backwards, however. Once we have become unfettered from a fervent fundamentalist-style faith through a thoughtful and critical approach to our tradition, there is no way to return to what the late Jesus scholar Marcus Borg calls "pre-critical naiveté," unless one undergoes serious head trauma or develops an intellectually crippling form of dementia. Ignoring what we have learned is disingenuous and downright pathetic. At the same time, we must find a way to create an accessible and palatable religious worldview without falling into a deeper hole of stupidity. How do we avoid being overwhelmed with too much information while simultaneously escape being underwhelmed with too little information?

Let's use the analogy of eating a meal. A large bite can cause choking and poor digestion. I suggest this is the current state of Christianity. We are being force fed large bites of theology—good or bad for us—effectively choking our faith and spirituality. When we try to talk/proclaim our faith with full mouths, no one can understand us. We're just spitting on people. We can't digest everything we are being forced to chew, so we become spiritually unhealthy. We are theologically bloated and overweight, consuming creeds, confessions, and statements of faith, not to mention tomes from some of the greatest minds in history, which is the equivalent of buffet meals at the local food trough. Eyeing a twelve-course meal might be exciting and even inspiring, but it's not good for us in the long run. What we need to do, theologically speaking, is consume smaller "lite bites," allow time for digestion, and then go walk it off. There is always more to chew on when the body needs it.

EFFICIENCY

Long before there was Elon Musk's DOGE (Department of Government Efficiency), there was the Department of God's Efficiency. Christianity Lite focuses on efficiency, although unlike Musk's department, it doesn't *cut everything*. In terms of efficiency, we're not there yet, but Jesus and his early followers gave it a shot. For centuries, the Israelites had suffered under the thumb of heavy and inefficient religious practices. Headquartered at the Temple in Jerusalem, Israel practiced a sacrificial system. To get "right with God," people brought their animals to be slaughtered and burned and their crops to be charred on the altar. Unless the priests who performed these sacrifices supplemented their income as chefs at a local restaurant, this was a wasteful and impractical system. Unless the animals and crops were on the menu that day and were just cooked rather than burned, this is inefficiency at its worst. It was a waste of nutritious food in a place where hunger and malnutrition were a serious problem.[19]

I'm not the only one who thinks the sacrificial system was wasteful and cumbersome. So did Jesus. Remember when he comes to the Temple in Jerusalem, possibly at the beginning of his ministry (according to John's gospel) and/or at the end of his ministry (according to Matthew, Mark, and Luke's gospels)? He is so irked by what he sees that he upends the moneychangers' tables and drives out the sacrificial animals. To him, this system is gross and grossly wasteful. And because he creates such a big commotion in the Temple, he ends up on a Roman cross.

His early followers have a dilemma: How do they interpret the meaning of Jesus' death? One of his followers in the late first century, the author of the letter to the Hebrews, comes up with a clever answer. He claims Jesus takes on a DIY or do-it-yourself project. Jesus effectively puts an end to the wasteful and inefficient sacrificial system by 1) taking on the role of high priest, and 2) sacrificing himself. Don't miss how radical this theory is. The writer of Hebrews is upending the centuries-old sacrificial system just as Jesus upended the tables of the moneychangers.

Jesus and his followers are critical of more than just the sacrificial system. They are also critical of the inefficiency of the Law of Moses; only the few people who could read in that time and place, such as the scribes, are familiar if not knowledgeable of the laws or commandments and thus can obey them. Jesus knows that the Law of Moses is inaccessible and overwhelming for most of the people. It doesn't work for them, but it works for the scribes, so just as the Temple priests have a vested interest in keeping the sacrificial system afloat, the scribes have a vested interest in keeping the Law of Moses front and center.

One day, a scribe approaches Jesus to see how knowledgeable he is about the Law. He knows that if he can expose Jesus's ignorance about the Law, the people will no longer trust him, and they will stop following him. Trying to trick him, he asks Jesus, "Which commandment is the first (or most important) of all?" Much to the chagrin of the scribe, Jesus gives a well-reasoned answer. As noted earlier, he funnels all six hundred and thirteen laws or commandments—most of them ridiculously cumbersome—down

---

19. I suspect most of it was burned to ashes because they believed that the smoke rising from the burnt offerings made it to God's nostrils. That's kind of a creepy image of God, is it not? If I were a comedian, I could imagine God taking a sniff and proclaiming, "This aroma is delightful! You are forgiven!"

to two: Love God and love neighbor. He even gets the scribe to admit this is a good answer and that "this is much more important than all whole burnt offerings and sacrifices."[20]

In one brief story, Jesus manages to dismantle the power of the two primary and most powerful religious institutions in ancient Israel: the sacrificial system and the Law of Moses. He does this because he is focused on efficiency. He has no use for religious practices that are wasteful, overwhelming, impractical, cumbersome, heavy-handed, and inefficient. We should follow suit. Love God, love neighbor. No silly laws need to be followed; no animals need to die—unless they are on tonight's menu.

HYBRIDITY

Jesus is a troublemaker. He regularly finds himself in conflict with those who disagree with his Sabbath activities, such as allowing his hungry disciples to pluck heads of grain from a field or healing on the Sabbath. He isn't even trying to hide what he is up to. Unfortunately, the Pharisees, men who see themselves as the final authority on their religious laws, are not impressed. They believe that doing anything on the Sabbath, including feeding and healing human beings, is an act of disobedience against God, so they seek his destruction. In his brief ministry, Jesus was up against a heavy-handed expression of faith I call "purebred religion." Purebred religion is uncomfortable mixing other perspectives, allowing a little wiggle room, bending a few rules, or making compromises for the sake of people. The Pharisees use words like "impure," "unclean," and "unholy" to describe those who "color outside the lines" on occasion. Jesus loved coloring outside the lines.

The word "Pharisee" means "separated one." Just as some people don't like the different foods on their plates touching one another, the Pharisees did not want other religious perspectives to come into close contact with theirs. Although their ancestors had mixed and assimilated with other religions to survive, they believe they are now at a point where they have something that needs to remain pure, unmixed, and uncontaminated. But then, amid this purebred religiosity comes Jesus and his hybrid approach to religion. Unlike the "separated ones," Jesus doesn't mind mixing it up with others. Other than feeding and healing people on the Sabbath, he wanders around the countryside touching or contacting unclean lepers, corpses, and women. All taboos. He becomes friends with traitorous tax collectors,

---

20. Mk. 12:28–34.

sinners of all kinds, and gentiles, he heals the demon-possessed, the blind, the lame, and the deaf, breaks dietary and handwashing laws, eats with anyone and everyone, and defiles the Temple. All of this is an impure, unclean, and unholy activity. His is the opposite of purebred religion, which appeals to us because we live in a world of hybrids. We are comfortable with combinations and compromises, mixtures and moderation, blending and balance. We enjoy a colorful world rather than a world in black and white.

The word "hybrid" is an early seventeenth-century Latin word that referred to such things as "the offspring of a tame sow and a wild boar, or a child of a freeman and slave."[21] Hybrids exist in every corner of creation, from plants to animals to people. In some sense, people of "mixed race," which includes all of us, are hybrids. My predominant ancestry is a hybrid people called "Scots Irish." We didn't come up with a very creative name for ourselves. We take all this for granted because we live in one of the most "mixed salad" or "melting pot" countries in the world.[22] Americans as a people are the result of the integration of multiple immigrant influences. Even our language is a hybrid language, borrowing and combining words from our cultural ancestors and neighbors. Hybridity is everywhere we look—in our Tex-Mex food, our rockabilly or Country rap music, and even in our golf clubs.[23] Of course, when we hear the word "hybrid," we immediately think about those automobiles that combine an electric motor with a gasoline engine.

There is hybridity in religion as well, which Jesus clearly practices by taking away the illusion of ritual and religious purity. He introduces color into a black and white world. His flexible faith is rooted in love and compassion rather than laws and codes. "The Sabbath was made for humankind, and not humankind for the Sabbath," he says.[24] The separated ones disagree. Exodus 20:8 says "Remember the Sabbath day, to keep it *holy* (i.e. pure and clean). Six days you shall labor, and do all your work, but the seventh day is the Sabbath of the Lord your God." Does this really mean

---

21. "hybrid," s.v. "hybridas, *New Oxford American Dictionary* (noun or adjective), http://www.oed.com.

22. "Mixed salad" refers to living next door to people of other ethnicities and cultures, whereas "melting pot" refers to the consequence of cohabitating and reproducing with one another. Amoskala, "The Meling Pot vs. the Salad Bowl."

23. One of the most disturbing things I have ever witnessed is the creation of hybrid golf clubs, which is a wood that is designed to go the same flight and distance as an iron club. That's just too much change for me to handle.

24. Mk. 2:27.

that one should not be allowed to glean from a field or heal someone on the Sabbath? The Pharisees think so; Jesus does not.

Jesus is motivated by compassion; the Pharisees, like contemporary purveyors of traditional Christianity, are motivated by cleanliness. They want to maintain a purebred religion, one with no wiggle room, no flexibility, no gray area, no alternative interpretations, no compromises, and thus, no compassion, even for those who are hungry or hurt. Hybrid religion, a manifestation of Christianity Lite, is messier than purebred religion, yet its flexibility, limberness, and openness allow room for a fuller expression of love and compassion. Hybrid religion can worship in whatever way it chooses—traditional, contemporary, or blended worship. It can worship online or onsite, indoors or outside, in casual dress or formality. It can pray with heads down or up, sitting on hands or waving them in the air. It can practice rituals and rites from tradition or borrow from others. It can consist of, as a colleague of mine calls us, "hyphenated Christians."[25]

A HEAVY ISSUE: BINARY OR SPECTRUM THINKING?

One method people have employed since the beginning of time to lighten their thinking load, to simplify matters and conserve time and energy, is to engage in binary or "black and white" thinking.[26] Some folks suggest binary thinking should be a thing of the past, a dusty relic, a type of thinking that should have disappeared the minute humanity began stringing coherent thoughts together. At best, binary thinking is simplistic and naïve, and at worst misleading and manipulative. That's a fair point. The *Urban Dictionary*, a product of contemporary "wokeness", delivers a near fatal blow to binary thinking by defining it (and criticizing it) as "A system of thought that predominantly considers things in an 'either, or,' 'right, wrong,' 'black, white' way, ignoring any subtleties or consideration of . . . more alternatives. In philosophy, this is known as a 'bifurcation fallacy.' People who habitually think in this way are usually . . . unintelligent and unimaginative."[27]

My response to this definition and critique of binary thinking is, "yep, that's true," however, it is also true that absolutist criticisms of binary

---

25. Snider, ed., *The Hyphenateds*.

26. I fully comprehend that the phrase "black and white thinking" can be interpreted as a racially charged micro-aggression, but I use it solely to help define what is now commonly referred to as "binary thinking."

27. "binary thinking," *Urban Dictionary*, http://urbandictionary.com.

thinking tend to err in the same manner as binary thinking itself. Even as we strongly denounce it, we do so by committing the same fallacy, or at least it feels that way to me. There is no question that binary thinking can lead to irrelevant or even dangerous conclusions. It can divide us and create more extremist views, which is evident and obvious in twenty-first century American politics. Binary thinking often offers arbitrary if not false choices. It narrows the list for the sake of convenience; thus, we need to make certain that the list is long enough to include every point that needs to be made.

Spectrum thinking, in contrast, considers multiple options, alternatives, and possibilities. Spectrum thinking uses less black and white and more multiple shades of gray if not color. It gives us more nuance than binary thinking, it is more dynamic and open to change, although at times it creates such a complex web of information that it effectively stymies the thinker. There is a reason why binary thinking is our default setting. It is more accessible to people than spectrum thinking. When one is squeezed for time or limited in resources, one looks for a simple, quick, and handy solution to a problem or issue. If one is writing a dissertation, one must employ spectrum thinking if one desires a good grade, but most of us, most of the time, are not writing dissertations.

Due to our lack of time, energy, intelligence, or motivation to dive into the deep end of the pool of theology and other related disciplines, those who complain about, criticize, and look down their noses at folks engaged in binary thinking need to go outside and breathe some fresh air. They need to step across their bubble's threshold. Yes, the world would be better off if people engaged in more grayish and colorful nuanced spectrum thinking but let us remember that we evolved to be a species that, when faced with an immediate existential threat, narrows our choices down to two: Fight or Flight.[28]

Religion is, at its base, a natural response to existential threats. Religions evolved to help humanity engage in a "fight" against such things as death, evil, sin, and suffering. The positive aspects of religion have developed despite our natural tendency to fight against these dark forces. The focus on love, for example, is a result of thoughtful people who feel the need to lure humanity into a more nuanced and productive world. I clearly

28. If we have more time, energy, intelligence, and motivation, we can respond in other ways, such as negotiation or diplomacy, camouflage or "playing possum," or just accepting the outcome of the inevitable threat. We always have choices, even if there are no good possible outcomes.

understand calls from more academically oriented folks to compel people to think more critically about faith and social issues, although I can hardly imagine walking up to a Walmart shopper to ignite a conversation about, say, capital punishment, with depth, layers, nuance, and context.[29] From my vantage point, the average Christian perspective is prone to simplistic binary thinking that is awash with overly-biased assumptions about truth and reality. Metaphorically speaking, our crayon box is full of only black and white crayons. Our worldview is often "us vs. them".

Take the abortion debate as an example. People are labeled as either "pro-life" or "pro-choice." Critics of the former assume that "pro-life" is code for "pro-birth and, after that, you're on your own." Critics of the latter assume that "pro-choice" is a masked "pro-abortion" perspective, as if women are anxious if not gleeful to get the procedure. Most thoughts and feelings about abortion lie somewhere in the proverbial "muddy middle" where a lack of clarity and consensus continues to reign supreme. My own perspective about abortion, freely borrowed from the Clintonian approach, is that abortion should be "safe, legal, and rare."[30] For various reasons, this middling perspective does not sit well with binary thinkers on either side.[31]

There are a variety of ways Christians have painted themselves into binary corners. Denominationalism is the most obvious way we have set ourselves apart from one another. Denominations are largely the result of conflict. The two primary choices are: "fight"— "I will stay and fight to change/save my denomination"—or "flight"— "I will leave and join/begin another sect." These two responses almost always stem from "fright"— "I am worried about the fundamentalists/liberals taking over." From these primitive instincts, tens of thousands of Christian sects or denominations have arisen. Practically every denominational or sectarian expression of

---

29. I do not wish to disparage Walmart shoppers. I just mean to refer to anyone who is out in public per se. But yeah, diving into issues in real depth might not be the modus operandi of folks who are willing to sacrifice quality for quantity at the big box store.

30. Bill Clinton speech, C-Span, January 22, 1993.

31. "My body, my choice" and "abortion is murder" are examples of how binary thinking has become the norm in the abortion debate. I have learned that a good place to jumpstart a conversation about issues in a critical way is to roll out the Clinton doctrine in response to other major social issues as well. Guns? Due to the reality of how many people already have guns, we should work to make them safe, legal, and rare. Marijuana use? Safe, legal, and rare. Gender reassignment? Safe, legal, and rare. War? Safe for civilians, declared only by legal authorities, and extremely rare. The Clinton doctrine does not work with every social issue, but in many cases, it can help us move beyond binary thinking.

Christianity in history began as a simple opinion that hardened into a solid "truth". This, in turn, leads to a schism. In its formative stage, schisms are rooted in a single oppositional or wedge issue, such as *sola scriptura* or "we support marriage as only between a man and a woman," and then expands to include other doctrines or theological assertions that support the initial wedge issue. Denominational splits or schisms are thus born in the petri dish of binary thinking—two "chromosomes" split and go their separate ways, acquiring wholly different identities as the years and centuries go by.

Where does this leave us? Clearly, most people are not going to learn, develop, or engage solely in spectrum thinking any time soon. Ironically, spectrum thinking is *heavy* thinking, although preferable to binary or *light* thinking. At the same time, the ability to incorporate both types of thinking—binary for immediate time-constrained reactions, and spectrum for more thoughtful time-consuming responses—is preferable to exclusively one or the other.

2

God

PLAYING THE GOD CARD

Talking about God might not be as dangerous as risk-taking explorers entering uncharted territory because theologians have already provided us with compasses to give us direction and flashlights to see the path more clearly. Still, it is always possible that one will get lost venturing into the topic of God. We might lose our way, lose our footing, slip and fall, and sustain an injury or two. Nevertheless, nothing ventured, nothing gained. Because some unnamed and mysterious force may have implanted in us a gene or two that spurs curiosity and theological creativity, it is a risk that we gladly take.

I won't say too much about God—and certainly not anything that hasn't already been said before—and yet I do believe there are two general approaches to God-thinking or theology that I have labeled "God Heavy" and "God Lite." God Heavy is the God most of us are familiar with. This is a God that is all-powerful and controlling, as well as separate and distant. This default theological setting presumably "works" for millions of people, but one does not journey through life thinking about and relying upon God Heavy without a few pitfalls and pratfalls along the way. As our sages have said to us: The bigger they are, the harder they fall.

God Heavy is the "God Card" people are prone to play at a moment's notice. To "play a (fill in the blank) card" is a figure of speech that refers to a way to get an upper hand in a conversation. It is often used to gain an advantage in an argument or debate with someone.[1] Think of the cards you have been dealt in your life that have given you an advantage over others

1. I have played my ordination and PhD cards on many occasions, but to no avail.

in some way or another. Maybe you have played the boss card, the parent card, the wealth card, or the experience card. Anything that gives you an advantage. And then there are the cards that people play when they feel they are at a disadvantage. These cards are often played out of necessity, if not a sense of desperation, such as the race card, the gender card, or the victim card. For the most part, I am not bothered when this happens because my general philosophy is that we should play the cards that are dealt to us if our intentions are good, and our cause is just.[2] And then there is the "God card." When, if ever, should we play the God card? I have a few observations to share:

First observation: When we Christians are accused of believing in three gods—Father, Son, and Holy Spirit—we like to play the God as Trinity card. The Trinity is one of the most difficult doctrines in the Christian faith. It is almost impossible to explain. In fact, I once had a professor who told us that every attempt in history to explain Trinitarian theology has been declared a heresy at one time or another by some ecclesiastical body of authority. When we play the Trinity card, we must be ready for some confused looks and critical responses.

Second observation: Many people enjoy playing the God Spoke to Me card. This is also known as the God Told Me To card, the God is Leading Me card, or the I Feel that God Wants Me To card. We should be careful playing these cards. At best, playing the God Spoke to Me card is an expression of our faith and passion about the important role God plays in our lives. At worst, playing the God Spoke to Me card can be manipulative, a heavy-handed power play to get one's way. To speak with absolute certainty about what we feel is God's will in our lives can be self-serving. If we play the God Spoke to Me card, we should do so with as much humility as we can possibly muster.

Third observation: Throughout history, the most frequent way people have played the God card is to explain Creation. This is the God is Creator card. After all, we need some kind of explanation for the existence of the universe. One of my favorite philosophical questions is, "Why is there something rather than nothing?" In response to that, theologians usually play the God is Creator card. This was especially true in the ancient world before the advent of science.

---

2. My favorite card, which I have yet to play, but I keep in my back pocket, is the Monopoly "Get out of Jail Free Card." For obvious reasons, I never leave home without it.

The book of Genesis plays the God is Creator card; twice actually, because there are two different Creation stories in the first couple of chapters of Genesis. On Day One in the first story, God created light, which is appropriate because the most ancient origin of the word "divinity" meant "to shine."[3] Divinity is that which shines. So, God's first act of Creation was divinity doing what divinity does: shine. After light is created, God can then *see* to create everything else: the sky, land, seas, vegetation, sun, moon, and stars (weirdly, created after light), birds, sea creatures, wild and domestic animals, and humans bearing God's image. Interestingly, the first card God gives humanity to play is the Dominion card, a card we are still playing, sometimes for good and sometimes for ill.

In the last few hundred years, a little thing called "science" came along, shaking the foundation of the Creation story. Is it possible to reconcile science and religion? Personally, I have no problem playing both the science and the God is Creator cards to explain the origin of, and ongoing workings of the universe. What we should avoid, however, is playing the God is Creator card only when the science card doesn't work. We can't just fill in the gaps of scientific knowledge with the God is Creator card. We shouldn't just play the various God cards when we think we have no other choice. Maybe we shouldn't think about God as a card at all, a card we play only when we need God. Maybe we should think of God as the whole deck of cards.

THE POWER OF PERSUASION

We also tend to play the God Card when life is kicking our proverbial asses, although believing and trusting in a theistic God is not always so easy, especially amid evil and suffering, which is a constant. If you have ever talked with an avowed atheist, a struggling agnostic, or even a critically minded Christian, the one excuse for *not* believing in God you will likely hear coming from their lips is this: If there is an all-loving, all-knowing, and all-powerful God, why is there so much evil and suffering in the world? This is a huge stumbling block or obstacle to faith for many people. Maybe the hugest. In his essay, "Good, Freedom, and Evil," the prominent Christian philosopher, Alvin Plantinga, famously called the problem of suffering "the only good objection to God."[4] This is the ultimate faith conundrum. Because of evil and suffering, it is difficult to be a faithful, trusting believer.

3. "Divinity," *Online Etymology Dictionary* (noun), http://www.etymonline.com.
4. Plantinga, *God, Freedom, and Evil*, 30.

Since Day One, religious people of all stripes have grappled with the imperfections of humanity and nature.

The early Christians, of course, were no strangers to evil and suffering, and yet the Apostle Paul came up with a nifty way to not allow evil and suffering to get in the way of faith and trust in God. In Romans 8:18, Paul daringly claims that "the sufferings of this present time are not worth comparing with the glory about to be revealed to us." That's an inspiring quote, but let's reflect on it for a moment. Paul is declaring that all the suffering in the world—in every present moment—does not measure up to the incalculable glory that will be revealed to us in the future—whatever that is. Can we calculate the math? You and I have limited knowledge of the sum of all suffering. I can't begin to imagine, for example, the extent of the pain and suffering of just the victims of the Holocaust or slavery or the war in Ukraine or the recent pandemic. I can't even imagine the pain of losing a single child. Paul's claim is bold and audacious. It has the distinct odor of theological exaggeration. Hopefully, Paul is right, and yet I'm not sure how convincing and comforting this is for someone who has just experienced unimaginable evil, trauma, or suffering: "You lost your family in the war? No sweat. The glory that will be revealed to you will make your current suffering feel less painful than a stubbed toe." I'm not sure that argument works.

To claim to have an answer to the problem of evil and suffering is entirely pretentious. Philosophers and theologians have been trying to come up with an answer for millennia. Nevertheless, I might as well give it a go. Here is my answer, one that reflects a theologically lite touch: If there is evil and suffering in the world, it is almost impossible to defend all three claims about God, that God is all-loving, all-knowing, and all-powerful. To do so would require a great deal of "mental gymnastics." It doesn't add up. Something's got to give. Therefore, what if we eliminate or change one of these three attributes?

First, should we change our view that God is *all-loving*? If God's children—us—are in any way a chip off the old block, then we could easily claim that God does not operate strictly out of love. There is a lot of hate and ill will among God's self-proclaimed children; we could say that we, the apples, do not fall far from the tree, therefore God is not as loving as we would like to believe. And yet, I can't give up my belief that God is all-loving. I would hate to live in a universe where the Creator might have a bad hair day and blow up the whole thing just for spite or kicks and giggles.[5] That might have worked in the Hebrew Scriptures a time or two, but it doesn't work any longer. Jesus points us toward a God with unlimited love. I'm going with that.

Second, should we change our view that God is *all-knowing*? Admittedly, we only know knowledge or knowingness from what's inside our narrow noggins. Whatever knowledge is to God, I feel certain that it is over our heads. Like way over our heads. God knows everything in a way that is infinitely incomprehensible to us. I would also hate to live in a universe where the Creator must go back to seminary on occasion for continuing education classes. So, no, I'm not willing to give up the notion that God is all-knowing either, at least in terms of knowledge of the past and present. In my opinion, to a large degree the future is unwritten and thus God's knowledge of the future can only be inexact.[6]

Finally, should we change our view that God is *all-powerful*? Here is where I think we have some wiggle room because I suggest there are two basic types of power in the universe. There is *controlling* power and there is *persuasive* power. Logically speaking, if God has controlling power, then we can rightly blame God for all the evil and suffering in the world. If God has the power to control everything, then God is ultimately responsible for evil and suffering, perpetrated by humanity or nature. God can stop it, but God doesn't—not all of it anyway. This suggests God is less moral than a police officer who witnesses a crime and does not attempt to stop it. I suggest that God does not have controlling power, which implies we need to be careful when we say, "God is in control." What do we even mean by that? Do we mean that God can control the violent impulses of the Putin's and Hitler's of the world or microscopic viruses that kill millions of people?

Rather than *controlling* power, I prefer to think that God has *persuasive* power. God is the ultimate influencer of the universe. In the social media world, an "influencer" is someone who has the power to affect people's purchasing decisions. An influencer doesn't make people buy things; they merely dangle the possibilities in front of the interested parties. They persuade people to buy things. This is what God's power is like from the perspective of Christianity Lite. God doesn't make us believe or trust; God

---

5. I'm ignoring some of the ancient mythologies, such as the story of Noah and the flood, where God does indeed have a bad hair day.

6. I suggest, however, that God knows all the potentialities of the future, just not the exactitudes, which is more awesome and mind-bending to me.

doesn't make us practice kindness or forgiveness or anything else Jesus taught. Instead, God persuades us to do these things. But how? I suggest that God's persuasive and influential power is expressed solely as divine love. Do you see what this implies? It implies that God's alleged attributes of being all-loving and all-powerful *are one and the same*. Love *is* God's power. God's power *is* love.

GOD AS TROUBLESHOOTER

We live in stormy times, literally and figuratively. Literally, hurricanes, typhoons, and cyclones are becoming stronger and more destructive because the oceans are warmer. Flooding is out of control. Winter storms are worsening. Heat waves are getting hotter and longer. Wildfires are rampant. We all have our own stories and battle scars inflicted by Mother Nature because we've all had to deal with her temperature tantrums due largely to our denial of climate change and subsequent negligence. Philosophers refer to the revenge inflicted on us by nature as *natural evil*. Natural evil is completely random with no thought behind it. When we add illness, accidents, and wild animals to the list of examples of natural evil, the list gets very long. In a very real sense, the universe, from microbes to meteors, is trying to get rid of us.

In addition to natural evil, there is *moral evil*, caused by the decisions and actions of human beings. This is evil created by folks who intentionally want to harm others. There is always someone or something lurking in the background ready to strike us or someone we love.

Due to the suffering humanity and creation endure both from the whims of nature and the willful behavior of human beings, I wonder if religion would even exist if somehow life was always peaceful, uneventful, and trouble-free. Did religion develop among early humans because they couldn't tame Mother Nature or their enemies? Was *troubleshooting* the original purpose of religion and the gods? After all, the ancient gods were all troubleshooters of some sort. Like the occasional mobster, they were "fixers." But what were they called upon to fix?

Folks in the ancient world generally believed in four types of gods:

1. Storm gods that have power over chaotic weather and nature
2. Warrior gods that lead their people into battle and victory

3. Fertility gods or goddesses that help with crops, livestock, and human reproduction
4. Healing and/or dying and rising gods (immortals) that are called upon to "fix" illnesses and overcome the power of death

Does any of that sound familiar? The ancient gods were troubleshooters. For the most part, the God of the Bible, as depicted in both the Old and New testaments, falls into one or more of these categories, depending upon the needs of the people.

What are we to make of that assertion? Is God our fixer? Is that what God does? Here we come to a faith fork in the road. We can go in one of two directions. First, we can choose to read the biblical accounts as if God can fix our *outside* problems, the consequences of natural and moral evil encroaching upon our lives. The problem with believing God will fix our outside problems is that when—not if—but when our outside troubles continue, we will become disillusioned with God and our faith in a "fixer God" will eventually fizzle out. God is not our "heavy," a mobster who carries a weapon with him to "fix" things.

The other direction we can take is to see God as the troubleshooter or fixer of what is happening on the *inside*. With God, it's always "an inside job." Here we see God as the one who stills the storms and kills the Stormtroopers that invade our hearts and minds, those things that create unnecessary fear, chaos, and turmoil in our innermost being.

This is where the believers in the ancient gods went astray. They understood the gods as troubleshooters or fixers of evil in the physical and material world. This is understandable because the outside world was even scarier and harsher for them than it is for us. They had little or no warning or control over bad weather or bad people. I would want my God to step in and fix these things too. What they should have concluded, however, is that God is the fixer of our *faith* and the troubleshooter of our *trust*. God is the One who fixes what is on the inside despite what is happening on the outside.

GOD IS PURT NEAR

Sometimes separation is a good thing. A marriage or relationship has become irreconcilable. Two dogs in a vicious fight need to be pulled apart. Booster rockets need to fall away from a space vehicle. An old band aid needs to be ripped off. You get the idea. Not all separation is bad. But then there is a thing called "separation anxiety." This is a diagnosed anxiety disorder in which someone with a strong emotional attachment to someone else is forced to separate from them for various reasons—first day of school, moving away, a broken relationship, a death in the family—and this separation leads to a high level of anxiety. Thomas Bayly, in his 1850 song, "The Isle of Beauty, wrote, "Absence makes the heart grow fonder." Does this mean that presence makes the heart grow indifferent? Does familiarity breed contempt, as is often said?

Anxiety or not, are we ever really separated from God's presence? This is an important theological question even for those who don't spend their afternoons in ivory towers. Many of Jesus's parables imply that God's so-called Kingdom is so subtle, so understated, and so inconspicuous, that we are largely unaware of it. When we think of the word "Kingdom," however, we think of sprawling castles, larger than life royals, and huge armies at their disposal. We think of size, power, and a dominating presence.

In contrast to that, Jesus characterizes the Kingdom of God as a tiny seed, something that we don't see as we are walking across a field until we are shocked to see a giant shrub. It's like yeast, a foreign element hidden in flour that helps the dough rise. It's like a treasure buried in a useless and forgotten field, hidden, unnoticed, until one solitary pearl is accidentally discovered, and then the owner recognizes exactly how precious the field is and has always been. It's like selling everything we own for one solitary pearl. It's like throwing a tiny net into a vast ocean and surprisingly finding fish "of every kind" in it. Jesus's parables are clever. Calling something subtle, understated, and inconspicuous a "Kingdom" is like calling a large man "Tiny" or a small dog "Bear" or "Moose." Jesus is trying to tell us that even though at first glance God's presence seems small and insignificant to us, it really isn't. We are always in God's presence, whether we are aware of it or not.

The Kingdom of God was on Jesus's mind from the very beginning of his ministry. If he had written a thesis for his Master of Divinity degree, the Kingdom of God would have been his topic.[7] In his first expression of the good news recorded at the beginning of Mark's Gospel, Jesus proclaims, "The time is fulfilled (now), and the Kingdom of God has come near."[8] In all

---

7. He might have been bewildered by the contemporary insistence to substitute "kingdom" with "kin-dom" because he is intentionally using a term that denotes power.

8. Mk. 1:15.

our attempts to formulate the gospel or good news, the simplicity of Jesus's message has always been as close to us as the top of our blurry unfocused noses: the Kingdom of God has come near. The Apostle Paul seems to have had similar thoughts about God's nearness. In Acts 17:28, Paul quotes the ancient Greek poet, Aratus, saying, "In him (God) we live and move and have our being." As the old cowboys might say sitting around a campfire, "That's purt near."

Is God "purt near" to us? If so, what does that mean? To help us answer this question, let's look at several different approaches to theology. The first one, called "theism" or "monotheism," is the traditional, heavy-handed Western and Near Eastern understanding. It is the one most of us grew up hearing sermons about, whether the preacher called it "theism" or not. We were raised on theism, which claims that God and the universe or creation, which includes you and me, are separate from one another. God created the universe (in six metaphorical days). Soon after that, sin entered the world, and because God is "holy," a gap emerged between God and all "fallen" creation, including humanity. God tried to close the gap between us with the Law, the teachings of the prophets, and various covenants, but was largely unsuccessful until Jesus emerged and managed to bridge the gap between God and humanity/creation. This is what theism looks like. God might be close to us in this worldview, thanks to Jesus, but I keep hearing the old adage echoing in my head: "Close only counts in horseshoes and hand grenades."

If theism's brand of "nearness" doesn't work for you, there is a lesser-known theological worldview called "panentheism," which literally means "all in God." Everything that exists, exists within God's realm. The universe is in God. Bridging a gap is unnecessary because no gap exists.

There are other theological worldviews, such as "pantheism," which means "all *is* God." According to an oversimplification of pantheism, you and I and the pews and the candles and the birds and the trees outside are divine. I suspect this sounds a little weird to most folks who are not inclined to see armadillos as divine.

A fourth option is "polytheism," the view that there are many gods, all separate from us. I suspect this also sounds weird to those of us who grew up in a "One True God" environment. I have always assumed there's only room for *one* "One True God." I can't imagine a couple of disputing supreme beings meeting at high noon in the cosmic town square, as one of them says to the other, "This universe ain't big enough for the both of us!" That's just silly to me.

A fifth option is "deism," which teaches that God created the universe and then went away on a permanent cosmic vacation. As large as the universe is, sightseeing must be amazing.

All of this might be a little confusing, but it does compel us to ask, "Can we ever be separated from God? Not according to Paul, who, in Romans 8:38–39, writes, "For I am convinced that neither death, nor life, nor angels, nor rulers, nor things present, nor things to come, nor powers, nor height, nor depth, nor anything else in all creation, will be able to separate us from the love of God in Christ Jesus our Lord." From a Christianity Lite perspective, we have never been and never will be separated from God's love. There is nothing we have done, are doing, or will do, that separates us from God's love. The Kingdom of God might be subtle, understated, and inconspicuous, but it is always purt near to us.

THEOLOGY ON TURF

The gist of the Bible, written by and for downtrodden, demoralized, and defeated people, is patience and hope, perseverance and determination, triumph and victory. It is a guidebook—a playbook—for overcoming chaos, the opponent of *shalom*. One story after another features a defeated team that goes by various names: the Hebrews, the Israelites, the Jews, the Christians—all experiencing one bad losing streak after another. All that's needed is a good coach and a few good draft picks. One imagines these teams sitting dejectedly in their locker rooms after every defeat, complaining about bad calls, bad luck, or bad coaching. From the Assyrian conquest and dispersion of the Israelites in 722 B.C., to the Babylonian conquest and exile of the Judeans in 586 B.C., to the Roman occupation of Jewish Palestine and the destruction of the Temple in 70 A.D., to the persecution of the early church in the late first century, the Bible is a panorama of chaos.

But there's always hope. That's the message of the Bible. The first story in scripture, the Creation myth in Genesis 1, where God creates order out of chaos, is spot on. It sets the tone for what will occur all throughout biblical history and even today . . . because if there is one appropriate word to describe the News today and always it is the word "chaos." I also like to use the word "mayhem," so I tend to see the Bible as a manual for overcoming mayhem. I enjoy those Allstate insurance commercials that feature the actor, Dean Winters, portraying "mayhem" . . . "like me," he says, with an evil twinkle in his eye. Insurance, of course, is a recent invention. The people who lived in the world of the Bible didn't have insurance. Rarely did they even have a stable society. It was one potential moment of chaos and mayhem after another. But they did have the God of scripture. And what was the God of scripture doing from one page to the next? Defeating the forces of chaos and mayhem in the world.

It all began on that first day of the season, poetically described as the beginning of Creation in Genesis 1. Here we can reimagine the Creation story as the transformation of a bad football team into a good football team. This is the story of the beginning of the championship run of the Hebrew Wilderness Wanderers, led by a rising star in the coaching fraternity named Yahweh. In the beginning, Coach Yahweh's team is a vapid roster of unskilled players. They are drowning in chaos. They are swept away in every game they play. In those early years, their biggest crosstown rival is the Canaanite Chaos, led by their coach, Baal. Baal's team features a trio of superstars named "Thunder," "Lightning," and "Stormy Weather." No one can beat them in an outdoor stadium. Your only chance is to get them indoors.

The Hebrew team is so bad, coach Yahweh is anxious for draft day because he gets the first pick. His first-round draft selection is a blue-chip quarterback named "Light." Light is a very bright player. Immediately, the difference in Yahweh's team is like night and day. A good quarterback will do that.

The coach's second round draft pick is a tight end with great height and vision, named "Sky," a player with unlimited potential. As his fans like to say, "The Sky's the limit."

In the third round, he picks two players, first a solid running back named "Earth." This should improve their ground game. Then he selects a defensive back that seems like he can cover the entire field at once, named "Sea." His fans in the stands invented the "wave".

In the fourth round, Coach Yahweh has the luxury of selecting two pass rushers named "Sun" and "Moon." His scouts had determined that the Sun can really bring some heat, while the Moon shines in a backup role.

In the fifth round, the coach selects a running back named "Sea Creature" who is difficult to bring down because he can slip out of any tackle. He will make a big splash when he comes into the league. Later that round the coach drafts a wide receiver named "Winged Creature." That guy can literally fly down the field.

Finally, in round six, Coach Yahweh has a couple more draft picks at his disposal. He begins with a safety named "Wild Animal," a very unpredictable player with good instincts. He's always swarming to the ball. His off-field behavior isn't the best, so they give him a curfew and put him in a cage at night. In the sixth round he also selects "Cattle," a beefy offensive lineman who loves playing on grass.

Toward the end of the draft, Coach Yahweh knows there is still a missing piece to his team. He confers with his scouts, the angels, who have been flying from game to game looking for potential talent. They tell him about a relatively unknown player named "Humankind." Humankind isn't very big, strong, or fast, but he is very cerebral. The coach decides this guy will make a great player-coach and decides to make him his play caller, giving Humankind "dominion" over the rest of the team.

And now you know the rest of the story . . . Yahweh's team goes on an unlikely championship run that far exceeds the legacy of Tom Brady and the New England Patriots. The coach has had some great players along the way: Moses, Deborah, Abraham, Sarah, Jacob, Esther, David, Hagar, Isaiah, Ruth, Jeremiah, to name a few. Twice, they build a huge stadium in Jerusalem that Jerry Jones envies, called the "Temple".

Unfortunately, as the years go by, they go back to their losing ways. Their main rivals are the Roman Gladiators who play their home games in the Colosseum in Rome, and the Herodians, who have taken over the Temple. Yahweh's team no longer has a home stadium, so they are practicing in the offseason near the Jordan River. The team is now down to one star player, a former water boy named John the Baptist.

Luckily, Coach Yahweh has a new draft pick coming soon that will bring his team back to prominence—Jesus of Nazareth. This guy can literally do no wrong. The scouting report on Jesus is that you can knock him down, but he will get right back up. Oh yeah, and he happens to be the coach's son.

3

Jesus

JESUS AS FISHHOOK

THE CHURCH HAS ALL-TOO-OFTEN used Jesus as a sledgehammer, a manipulative and coercive way to promote Christian superiority and exceptionalism. "No one comes to the Father except through me" is John's way of characterizing Jesus as the "Heavy."[1] One can almost hear this Jesus say to his adversaries, "Over my dead body." Fortunately, there are other less threatening ways to interpret and utilize the doctrine of Christology. I will begin by using the "fishhook" analogy.

My family has an extensive collection of Christmas tree ornaments. Almost every ornament on our tree has a story to tell or some special meaning behind them. One day, as I was helping my wife decorate our tree, reflecting on the significance of the ornaments, I began to think theologically, focusing on the hooks rather than the beautiful ornaments. Without the hooks, I realized that the ornaments are basically useless, inexpensive, and fragile pieces of glass or plastic with very little practical purpose. Most of them are not designed to sit or stand on a mantel or a shelf. They come in shapes that are designed to do just one thing: hang from the branch of a Christmas tree. Once a year.

As I was thinking about these unremarkable, yet important, little hooks, a thought entered my mind: *Jesus is the hook*. Christmas ornament hooks look much like fishing hooks, and yes, the Christmas story is a fishing story of sorts. God went fishing for humanity, using love as the bait and Jesus as the hook. Coincidentally, when Jesus began his ministry, he first

---

1. Jn. 14:6.

caught a few, well, fishermen. And what did he say to these first disciples who just happened to be fishermen? "Follow me," he told Simon and Andrew as they were casting a net into the sea, "and I will make you fishers of people."[2]

Here's my perspective, straight from my rusty, smelly, grimy tackle box of theology: God uses the *lure of love* to bring us into or onto what I call "the Sod of God." But God needs a setting, a place, to cast that love. God needs a good fishing hole and of all the fishing holes that were in the right place at the right time, our story begins in a little backwater country in the Middle East. According to the mythology of the time, God chooses a little town called Bethlehem because it already has a reputation for producing a great hook. King David was born there a thousand years earlier, flawed and bent out of shape as he was. That hook is now rusty and less usable, so God decides to visit the same tackle store. A man and his expecting wife are there, by happenchance it seems. The mother gives birth to a baby future storytellers will call "God's beloved Son."

Although this little hook will not be ready to be attached to God's lure of love for a few decades, the Great Fisherman decides to test the waters and cast a line to see how the fish are biting. The old tackle box is opened, a bevy of angels are used as lures, and a few hungry shepherds are caught. The Great Fisherman is in "catch and release" mode, so the shepherds return to their flock. Years later, using Jesus as the hook, the Great Fisherman begins to catch people again, this time without throwing them back, what we call "catch and keep."

Comparing Jesus to a fishhook on a lure is one way to characterize the Christology of Christianity Lite. This contrasts with more heavy-handed methods of evangelism, such as using an explosive device ignited in the middle of the lake or river.

GOOD TROUBLE

Lest anyone get the wrong idea, Christianity Lite is not totally devoid of some "heavy shit." There is room for a little drama, if not violence. In the gospels, Jesus gets into "good trouble." Most of us know what being in "bad trouble" is about. The worst trouble I ever got into at home was the time I "borrowed" my dad's '65 Ford Falcon and picked up two trouble-making

---

2. Mt. 4:19. I'm aware that my fish hook analogy is a little off base because they fished with nets in that day, but I will "stick" with the hook analogy if that's okay with you.

friends who were in possession of a few bottle rockets. I drove them around our tiny town shooting the rockets out of the car windows. One of them found a man's backside as he was tending his garden. He called my parents. When I got home, I was in a heap of bad trouble.

We were not put on this planet to get into that kind of trouble. We were put here to get into what the late congressman and civil rights leader, John Lewis, called "good trouble," something he did numerous times.[3] As I read the Gospels, I detect that Jesus is always getting into good trouble. It all begins at his baptism, a ritual that has become (or it should become) the most revolutionary act in our faith tradition. Baptism is an act of rebellion, even if one is baptized as an infant. In that case, our parents are revolutionaries, knowingly or not. Unfortunately, we have largely sanitized the sacrament of baptism and turned it into a harmless ritual where no one gets hurt or no one gets into trouble, although the roots of Christian baptism are revolutionary, seditionist, rebellious acts of treason. The ministry of baptism, begun from the hands of John the Baptizer, was an uprising against the Temple religion in Jerusalem.[4] We are a little too close to the bad trouble of January 6, 2021, at the U.S. Capitol, but John's ministry of baptism, an insurgence against Jerusalem, was good trouble. Baptism should be identified as an act of troublemaking.

We have no idea how many folks John was able to persuade to walk into the waters of the Jordan, but one day Jesus of Nazareth comes to him for his "bath of initiation." How willing is Jesus to do this? Is he excited? Does he feel manipulated? Is this somehow forced upon him by powers real or imagined? I tend to think Jesus' baptism is not some teary-eyed event where the recipient emerges from the waters feeling euphoric and cleansed of sin. I tend to interpret his baptism as bordering on an act of violence, more like when mobsters take a victim into a restroom and force his head into the toilet to make him "understand."

I am not saying that Jesus is brutally forced into the water by two thugs pinning him down, but what he experienced that day is closer to being "forcefully guided" than thinking about it as a sweet little moment when a few gentle drops course their way through Jesus' hair onto his shoulders while everyone is standing around dabbing their tears and applauding. This is the God of Order re-creating Chaos—the chaos of the waters that God

---

3. John Lewis was arrested more than forty times during his civil rights activism, primarily during the 1960s. Zimet, "Finding a Way.".

4. John the Baptist was caught wet-handed.

violently tamed at the beginning of time. After all, John is the baptizer, and he is not exactly St. Francis of Assisi. Picture a wild man dressed in camel's hair, a man who eats wild locusts for sustenance and looks like the Q-anon shaman of January 6 infamy, the guy with the buffalo horns. Do not be mistaken; the way most of us think about that Q-anon guy, deservedly so, is how the leaders in the Temple in Jerusalem think about John the Baptist. The difference is, from our perspective, the buffalo horns guy was stirring up bad trouble whereas the camel hair guy is stirring up good trouble. But trouble it is. Eventually, it leads to the arrest and execution of both John and Jesus. For some folks in that day, John and Jesus are nothing but trouble.

Jesus' baptism is one of the most dramatic moments in all of scripture. John "guides" Jesus into the troubled water, perhaps a complete immersion, top to bottom, and when he is finally allowed to come up for air and wipe the water from his eyes he looks up and sees the heavens torn asunder. Have you ever seen the sky split apart? I can't imagine what that might look like, yet I know it would get our attention and make us wonder if maybe we had crossed a line with Almighty God. And then, while John, Jesus, and the stunned crowd of on-lookers are still in shock, not knowing how to respond to what they have just seen, a dove gently descends from the torn open sky, like it has been ceremoniously released from a cage for a wedding or a funeral. As everyone is expressing their "oohs and aahs," a Voice from the sky speaks. Is someone in trouble? Is this like the voice of a stern father yelling at his son for borrowing his car and shooting bottle rockets from the window? No. The Voice affirms the trouble, saying, "You are my Son, the Beloved; with you I am well pleased." Phew! No one is in trouble today! This father is very pleased with his son.

Or is he? Because immediately the dove, or rather, the Spirit drives Jesus out into the adjacent wilderness. *Drives Jesus out into the wilderness.* Without the assistance of a Ford *Falcon*. I picture the dove turning into a large menacing bird, like a falcon, using its talons to hook Jesus by the ear, drag him up out of the water and "guide" him into the desert. The stunned crowd continues to watch, not knowing how to respond, not wanting to get into trouble with the wild camel hair clad man or with the Voice that has torn apart the sky or with the sweet-looking but now menacing Spirit. Stay put, they tell one another. Do not move. Certainly, do not follow him. He must be in trouble.

Jesus has some interesting company while he ponders his fate in the wilderness for forty days. Satan is there, up to his old temptation tricks, which is his forte. Just ask Job. The wild beasts are with Jesus, which is a given if one is in the desert, with or without the falcon. Speaking of winged creatures, the angels are there to "wait" on him, although I do not envision this being anything like a five-star restaurant.

From this story we can see how the trouble begins. From the chaotic waters of baptism, a troubled Messiah emerges to see the ripped open sky above and is then led out into a wilderness that is red in tooth and claw. While there he considers how he will make trouble for the world. Good trouble. It doesn't sound like trouble, yet when he declares, using a few sparse words, "The time is fulfilled, and the Kingdom of God has come near; repent, and believe the good news," he knew he was in big trouble.

THE MOON LANDING

"But who do you say that I am?" Simon Peter answered, "You are the Messiah, the Son of the living God."[5] If Simon Peter were an astronaut and had landed on the moon, we might say that he took a giant step forward for all mankind and then took a step backward. He was initially right about Jesus' identity (according to Jesus), but then he was wrong. He's not alone in his confusion. For several centuries at the beginning of the Christian era, the debate over Jesus's identity uses up most of the oxygen in the room. From the fourth through the eighth centuries, all the top brass of Christianity come together at seven different ecumenical councils to discuss such matters. Can you imagine debating Jesus's identity for five hundred years? We're still doing it, which means that anyone who thinks they have it all figured out is a loony space cadet.

Some of the greatest theological minds in the history of the church have grappled with this issue. Nothing comes close to the amount of fuel we have consumed trying to find consensus on what seems like a simple question from Jesus to his disciples, "Who do you say that I am?" Of course, Simon, son of Jonah, a.k.a. Peter, was like that kid in elementary school who always had to be first in line. He says, "You know what, I'll give it a shot." Simon didn't know it at the time, but his answer was like a *moon*shot. It was all or nothing. In terms of what we call "Christology," the doctrine of Christ, this is the first time someone has exited earth's theological orbit. His answer is so inspiring that we even have a fancy name for it: "The Petrine Confession." Peter's confession.

5. Mt. 16:15–16.

I know a little about the Petrine Confession. I wrote my master's thesis on it. It's titled "The Religious History of Banias (biblical Caesarea Philippi, the setting for Simon Peter's confession) and its Contribution to an Understanding of the Petrine Confession."[6] I decided to write about the history of Banias after a six-week archaeological expedition there in the summer of 1988, representing Hardin-Simmons University in Abilene, Texas. The purpose of my thesis was to help us understand Peter's confession in the context of the religious history of that place.[7]

After hearing what his Jewish disciples have heard about him, that he, Jesus, is a reincarnation of either John the Baptist, Elijah, Jeremiah, or one of the other prophets of Israel, Jesus directs the question to his disciples, "But who do *you* say that I am?" Simon launches his soaring answer: "You are the Messiah, the Son of the Living God." To use the language of Neil Armstrong, Peter's confession was "one small step for a man, one giant leap for mankind."[8] But that's not the whole story, is it? It turns out that Peter's confession was "two steps forward and one step backward."[9]

After Simon's confession, Jesus responds with the enthusiasm of a Mission Control director after a moon landing: "Blessed are you, Simon, son of Jonah! For flesh and blood has not revealed this to you, but my Father in Outer Space" or something like that. In Jesus's mind, Simon has taken a couple of steps forward in his discipleship. He deserves a higher rank. Using a play on words, Jesus gives Simon a new name: "Peter" (*Petros* in the Greek) and on this rock (*Petra*) "I will build my church, and the gates of Hades will not prevail against it." Simon Peter became "the rock," long before Dwayne Johnson. He becomes the *foundation* for the church—the launch pad for Christianity.[10] Jesus then gives Peter "the keys of the Kingdom of heaven," which means he will be the guy who gets to hit the ignition switch and control the speed and direction of this new mission. The keys

---

6. It's not a New York Times bestseller, but I hear it is gathering dust in someone's New York cellar.

7. My most creative conclusion is that the people who lived in or traveled through that diversely populated region may have thought that Jesus was the Greek god Apollo because Apollo was known for doing some of the things Jesus was known for doing, such as healing. Apollo was very popular at the time among the non-Jewish locals. Coincidentally, we liked him enough to name a moon-landing spaceship after him.

8. Armstrong had not yet learned to use inclusive language at the time of his moon landing.

9. Read Mt. 16:13–23 to get the less "spacey" version of this story.

10. Peter and "petroleum" are linguistically connected. Coincidence? I think not.

to the Kingdom allow Captain Peter to bind or loose—close or open—the hatch to the USS Christianity as he sees fit.

Peter is doing great so far. He has taken two steps forward—a giant leap for mankind—but it doesn't take long before he takes a step backward. It's as if an asteroid hits him on the head or he takes a wrong turn at the International Space Station. As Peter is basking in the moonlight of his new rank and mission, he hears Jesus talk about what sounds like a potential crash landing. Jesus says he will suffer "at the hands of the elders and chief priests and scribes" and be killed. Houston, we have a problem. Mission Control informs Peter that he has failed to hear Jesus' entire flight plan, which includes a relaunching of the mission on the third day. As we know from the biblical account, Peter will one day witness Jesus ascend into the heavens like—you guessed it—an astronaut.

But at this moment, Peter doesn't understand what he has just heard from Mission Control about a new launch date, so, as Captain of the ship, he reprimands Jesus, saying, "God forbid it, Lord! This must never happen to you!" This is not part of the mission! Peter has just taken a step backward. He might be the new Captain of the ship, but he has forgotten that Jesus is the Admiral. Peter has misunderstood the nature of the messianic mission. His confession may have been a moonshot, but his rocket boosters don't have enough fuel to get the job done. Admiral Jesus says to him, "Get behind me, Satan! (You are acting like you live on the dark side of the moon). You are a stumbling block to me (like an asteroid belt), for you are setting your mind not on divine (or heavenly) things but on human (or earthly) things." This must have felt like a demotion.

Two steps forward, one step backward. That's Peter's pattern, and it holds true for most of his life. Sometimes he gets it right; other times he gets it wrong. But at least he tries. In addition to misunderstanding the messianic mission, there is an episode when he tries to walk on water as if gravity doesn't apply to him. And let's not forget that Peter originally believes gentiles are as unclean as aliens until the Spirit teaches him not to call anything or anyone unclean that God has declared clean.

Peter is very much like you and me, at least from the perspective of Christianity Lite. We don't always get it right. In our voyage with Jesus, sometimes we make it to the Launchpad, but our ship isn't ready for liftoff. Sometimes we get all suited up, but we forget to bring our air tanks. Sometimes we strap ourselves in our seats, and then we realize we forgot to bring the keys. Sometimes we can lift off, but we don't have enough fuel to fulfill our mission. Sometimes we make it to the moon, but the hatch won't open. In a nutshell, or rather a space module, this is how it is for followers of Christ.

THE PRIME DIRECTIVE

Continuing with the space them . . . I prefer *Star Trek* to *Star Wars*. I suspect this has something to do with my generation or I found it "fascinating"—to use Mr. Spock's favorite word—to know that if Captain Kirk led an "away team" to an alien planet or spaceship, everyone who was wearing a red shirt was going to die.

Although each series in the *Star Trek* franchise represents a different era in a fictional *Star Trek* future, as far as I know they all have one thing in common: Starfleet General Order No. 1--The Prime Directive. This is *Star Trek's* version of "the greatest commandment" that Jesus talks about in the gospels. If you aren't a Trekkie, you might not know what I'm talking about. So, for all of you who wasted your time watching *Star Wars* or doing other inconsequential things with your life, allow me to explain.

"Starfleet" is the fictional space force of the United Federation of Planets, which is headquartered (of course) on Earth.[11] Starfleet's General Order No. 1—the Prime Directive—prohibits Starfleet from *interfering* in the normal development of less technologically advanced species that are likely unaware of the existence of the United Federation of Planets. They were ordered to be incognito; to let nature take its course. If you have ever wondered why UFOs haven't made their presence known in a big way on our planet, it could be that they have their own version of the Prime Directive and have been told not to reveal themselves to us—or more likely aliens haven't actually paid us a visit.

Regardless of the truth about UFO's, let's put ourselves in their shoes.[12] What if the species we are observing on another planet is in a crisis and we know we can help? Wouldn't we intervene on their behalf? In a book titled, *The Ethics of Star Trek*, the authors suggest that the Prime Directive is like a Catch-22: while their mission is "to seek out new life and new civilizations" they are prevented from interfering with their lives or civilization, even if they see a need to take immediate action to help them.[13]

11. We just can't help thinking we are the center of the universe, can we?
12. Or whatever footwear they use—if they even have feet in the first place.
13. Barad, *The Ethics of Star Trek*, 123.

Star Trek does a good job dealing with complex moral and ethical dilemmas, which is the reason I enjoy it so much. It's no surprise, then, that the characters on these shows often ignore or work around General Order #1. The temptation to help a struggling species is just too great . . . which is exactly what the Christmas story is all about. God was watching us and mostly "holding back," but then decided a little *interference* in our spiritual development was necessary.

Two-thousand years ago, Earth is in a pre-technological and pre-scientific stage of development. People have very little knowledge of the universe. They know nothing about galaxies, supernovas, stars, planets, comets, meteorites, and black holes. They have no sense of how far away the sun, moon, or stars are. They believe these celestial bodies are just beyond our reach in the heavens, the abode of God, literally above us in the sky. If we climb to the top of a mountain, we might get lucky and run into the Divine One, which is why people built their worship sites on the "high places." The Temple, for example, is built on Mt. Zion and Moses receives the Ten Commandments on Mt. Sinai, where God was hanging out.

Human beings are not just technologically deficient in the ancient world; they are also *spiritually* deficient. They have been developing religious traditions in every corner of the world for thousands of years, but there was something missing. So, God has a decision to make. Obey or ignore the Prime Directive. Leave humanity to their own devices and let them advance spiritually at their own pace or *interfere* in their spiritual development.

According to the Christmas story, God decides to ignore the Prime Directive and interfere on their behalf. God has been working around General Order #1 for a very long time. If one takes the Old Testament stories literally, God has been interfering in the development of *home sapiens* from the very beginning, although there is some attempt to disguise God's self. In the Garden of Eden for example, the Old Testament's version of "First Contact," the first couple "hears" God's voice but doesn't seem to lay eyes on God. Eventually, they are removed from the Garden because they ate from a tree that gave them too much knowledge too quickly.[14]

From that First Contact with humanity, perhaps God begins to realize the wisdom of the Prime Directive, so in story after story in the Old Testament, God interferes in the progress of humanity sporadically and in small doses. No one is allowed to "see" God because to do so would be too

---

14. Gen. 3.

CHRISTIANITY LITE

overwhelming. There is occasional interference, however. Folks occasionally hear God's voice, Moses hears God speaking from a burning bush, and God leads the Israelites out of Egypt under the covering of a pillar of cloud and fire. God interferes directly by giving the Ten Commandments and the Law to the Israelites, but Moses gets most of the credit. God's "presence" abides in the portable Ark of the Covenant and then in the Temple. God speaks *through* prophets, who offer warnings and encouragement. Some folks dream dreams and have visions. In story after story, God just cannot avoid the temptation of interfering in the affairs of humanity. God constantly ignores the Prime Directive yet does so sporadically and in small doses.

So far, nothing has worked all that well, so God sends forth a trusted officer, an angel of the Lord named Gabriel, to make First Contact on three occasions. First, Gabriel visits a priest named Zechariah, to tell him that his wife, Elizabeth, will have a baby named John who will eventually prepare the hearts and minds of people for the coming of the Messiah.[15] Six months later, God sends Gabriel to the city of Nazareth, to inform a young unmarried girl named Mary that she will also have a son, named Jesus, who will *be* the Messiah.[16] The Prime Directive has been ignored, but most people are not aware. Not yet anyway.

Shortly before Mary's baby is born, God chooses an appropriate place for Gabriel's third First Contact, the little town of Bethlehem, the birthplace of Israel's greatest king, David. Mary and her betrothed, Joseph, are there for a census. After she gives birth and lays Jesus in a manger, Gabriel makes contact again. This time he is not alone. Luke says he has "a multitude of the heavenly host" with him. This "away team," to use *Star Trek* terminology—none are said to be clad in red shirts—appear from the heavens to a group of shepherds who are keeping watch over their flock by night. They tell the shepherds about the birth of the Messiah.

Again, so far God's contact with humanity has been limited—sporadic and in small doses. The world does not yet know about God's "visit" with humanity. But as we know, the story does not end there. Perhaps God is trying to be incognito by interfering through the guise of a baby boy born in a barn in Bethlehem. But it doesn't work. The cat's out of the bag. The need was too much to ignore. The temptation to interfere was too great, so First Contact became Forever Contact. God's love is stronger than any Starfleet

15. Lk. 1:5–25.
16. Lk. 1:26–38.

Prime Directive, any Guideline of the Galaxy, Standard of the Solar System, or Court Order of the Cosmos. God saw that we were in a spiritual crisis, so God sent an away team led by Officer Gabriel, and yes, God's own son (which is always a risky endeavor). That's the William Shatner version of the Christmas story.

If God ever ignores the Prime Directive again and sends Jesus back to us riding on the clouds as the biblical writers imagined, just make sure you aren't wearing a red shirt.

CHRISTOLOGY ON THE COURT

I am a mild sports fan. Some might call me a "fair weather fan," but that's not exactly true. Weather has nothing to do with my consistent apathy. I don't sit in front of a television set all day long and watch sporting events, but I do have an ESPN app on my phone, and I try to keep up with the big stories in most of the major sports. On occasion, I will watch a ball game, a match, or a tournament, but it doesn't consume my life. The aging process is the only thing that does that.

I'm always interested, however, in who wins the individual awards each year, such as MVP's, Rookies of the Year, or Comeback Players of the Year. Most of the awards given in professional sports are sensible. The awards seem to "cover all the bases" (pardon the pun). I can see why, for example, we have batting champions in baseball, Players of the Year in golf, and a Coach of the Year award for the coach that gets the most out of the least. I get all that, but the one that has always surprised me, the one that I hear about every year and wonder, "Why do we give an award for that?" is the NBA's *Sixth Man of the Year Award*.

This award has been given since the 1982–1983 NBA season to the league's best performing player for his team *coming off the bench* as a substitute (or sixth man). If you know only the bare minimum about basketball, you know there are only five people from each team on the court at any one time. Presumably, the five *best* players on a team are the ones who make up the starting lineup. The Sixth Man Award seems to be cheating the five starters out of a potential award they could put on their resume and use to negotiate for more money. I can envision, let's say, the fourth best player on a team walking up to the coach and saying, "Coach Jones, I'm never going to win the league's MVP award because I'm not even the best player on this team. But I'm obviously better than our first substitute off the bench who has a good chance to win the prestigious Sixth Man Award. So, can we switch spots? I would be happy to be the first player to come off the bench!" Am I wrong about this? Has anyone else ever wondered about the rationale for this award? I mean, why don't we award the best pinch hitter, pinch runner, or relief pitcher in baseball? What am I missing here?

Whether that award makes sense or not, there *is* something special about a person who comes off the bench to infuse a new level of energy into a game. In baseball we even use the word "save" to describe a relief pitcher helping his team hang on to a lead to win the game. In traditional renderings of the Gospel, this is exactly what Jesus does for humanity. He comes off the cosmic bench to lead us to victory. With that in mind, here's a reimagining of the Christian story:

God is the starting pitcher, throwing out the first pitch, which is so loud when it hits the catcher's mitt they called it the Big Bang. The starting lineup looks good, but then the first two players at bat, Adam and Eve, strike out. Afterwards, their son, Cain, is ejected from the game for unsportsman-like conduct. The angels in the outfield always play well, but that one rain delay hurts God's momentum, until a manager named Noah makes good use of his bullpen. The prophets of ancient Israel do their best to keep the game close by yelling at the umpires from time to time, but they keep getting ejected from the game as well. By then, God's fiercest opponent, Satan the Slinger, who can throw a real heater, begins to rack up the wins. God realizes something needs to be done. The top of his lineup, the Jews, have good RBI numbers (rabbis batted in), but the gentiles at the bottom of the order can't even find a jockstrap for the uncircumcised. Things are looking grim.

God goes to the bench and calls up his ace, who (as noted in the football analogy above) happens to be his own son, Jesus of Nazareth. Jesus gets the save. One of the most overlooked aspects of the Jesus story is that his name literally means "Yahweh saves." In the birth story we are told that the angel Gabriel (God's number one talent scout) is sent to a poor young unwed couple, Joseph and Mary, telling them they will have a son, *and you will name him Jesus*, "Yahweh saves." His very name suggests Jesus comes off the bench like a good sixth man in basketball, a relief pitcher, or a backup quarterback, and *saves* the game. Bring out the trophy!

At least, according to Matthew, Mark, Luke, and Paul's letters, Jesus comes off the bench. Depending on who you ask, various Christological formulas have him coming off the bench at different moments: at his birth, his baptism, or his Resurrection. According to John's Gospel and other New Testament writings, however, Jesus is always the "starter": "In the beginning was the Word, and the Word was with God, and the Word was God. He was in the beginning with God."[17] Jesus is God's Ace in that scenario. This gets even more interesting in Acts 1, in an event we call the "ascension," where Jesus is about to go back to the bench, like a pitcher triumphantly leaving the mound after a good outing. In this story, Jesus tells his new teammates, the Christians, that the Holy Spirit will now enter the game and re-energize them. Jesus says to them, "You will receive power when the Holy Spirit has come upon you," which is easier than hitting the gym every day.[18]

So, the next time you see someone come off the bench to save the game, think of Jesus. That way, you get to be a sports fanatic and a religious nut at the same time. You're welcome.

17. Jn. 1:1.
18. Acts 1:8.

4

The Holy Spirit

THE WAITING GAME

Much like traditional Christianity's understanding of God and Christ, the Holy Spirit is thought to force things to happen, like a heavy wind that blows over our trash cans. The Holy Spirit becomes an assault weapon in contrast to power that is organic, fluid, and subtle. Understanding Christianity Lite's view of the Holy Spirit's activity requires waiting and guessing. The Spirit operates in the context of the unexpected, unfamiliar, and inexplicable. Patience is required to "play the game" of the Spirit.

If we could describe our liturgical seasons in terms of a game, the season of Easter moving toward Pentecost is much like Advent—it's a *Waiting Game*. In Advent, we symbolically await the birth of the Christ child and after Easter we await the arrival of the Holy Spirit and the birth of the Church. To use an appropriate "birth" word, we are *expecting*. This is all play-acting and ritual because the Spirit is already here, just as the Christ child has already been birthed, and yet it is important to plug ourselves into the ancient stories to be reminded what this is all about. We learn best by rote. Therefore, we follow the path laid out for us like a Monopoly piece making its way around the board repetitively. We experience the flow of the liturgical seasons as if they are set up like a traditional board game. There is structure and instructions, repetition and rules, different liturgical colors around the board, and a goal, such as the arrival of the Holy Spirit and the birth of the Church. It's very much like a game, but of course it isn't a game.

Human beings love to play games. The moment *Homo sapiens* found a little free time in their daily struggle to survive, they began to invent games.

The Holy Spirit

Dice was invented about five thousand years ago. Now we have board games, card and domino games, sporting games, video games, role-playing games, mind games, and party games (beer pong, anyone?). The Olympics are even called "the Games," decorated with their own five differently colored rings: blue for Europe, yellow for Asia, black for Africa, green for Australia, and red for the Americas.

As we run up to Pentecost every year like an Olympic sprinter, we play a liturgical version of the Waiting Game, the same game the first disciples play as they wait for something unexpected, unfamiliar, and inexplicable. The book of Acts claims they are "all together in one place."[1] No doubt they are deep in prayer, and yet when they have some free time, I imagine someone moseys on over to a cabinet or closet and pulls out some board games. They are staying in a well-stocked Airbnb. I have no idea what board games they might have played to beat their boredom, but the game they are always playing, the game that prepares them for what is about to turn their world upside down, is the Waiting Game . . . and wait they do.

The Holy Spirit doesn't show up immediately after Jesus ascends into heaven. Jesus does not high-five the Holy Spirit as they pass one another in the clouds. They must wait another ten days, to add to the forty they have already endured. They need to sit in this Waiting Room, to prepare in prayer, commit to community, and wait in wonder for something unexpected, unfamiliar, and inexplicable. Turns out, the Holy Spirit is well worth the wait, especially if one appreciates fireworks and windy conditions. Nowadays we would have fire trucks on standby. If they had tried to launch a new religious movement before the Holy Spirit arrives with all that flair, Christianity would have spit and sputtered like an old car before it could even get started. So, they wait until, conveniently, the Day of Pentecost arrives, a day when everyone and their unleashed dogs are visiting Jerusalem.

Like the board games we used to play (before video games and smart phones), we can play them repetitiously. Board games can be pulled from the closet shelf at any time. The same for Pentecost and the Holy Spirit. The Holy Spirit doesn't just blow in and out leaving behind instructions on how to play the game of Christianity. Waiting is still the game. It's always the game. It is the game the Holy Spirit plays with us all the time, in every nook and cranny of our lives, and thankfully not according to our time preferences. If we want to be successful in the game of life—the actual game of

---

1. Acts 2:1.

life—we cannot impatiently force things to happen. "For everything there is a season and a time for every matter under heaven."[2] The Holy Spirit wrote that.

If the Holy Spirit's writing career had continued, I suspect we would have the following sacred words to ponder: "Spirituality (the Holy Spirit's modus operandi) does not consist of forcing square pegs into round holes. Spirituality consists of waiting for the Spirit to round out the edges of the pegs." Waiting is a spiritual discipline, and Christ's disciples are waiters, in more ways than one. They are waiters in terms of serving others, and they are waiters in terms of time. Tom Petty, the late great rock and roller from my youth, had it right: "The waiting is the hardest part."[3] No one chooses to play the Waiting Game. It chooses us. We don't play the Waiting Game because we want to. We don't play it *on* purpose. We play it because we *have* a purpose, and the purpose takes a while to percolate.

THE FLAME EFFECT

If there is one thing we can claim with some degree of credibility, it is that the Holy Spirit is helping us increase our spiritual intelligence, which is just one of many ways of being intelligent. A study of the so-called "Flynn Effect" shows that young people are, on average, more intelligent than the rest of us. I don't mean wiser—necessarily—because wisdom and advancing age tend to work well together, but I do mean smarter in terms of potential IQ. The Flynn Effect was named for the late James Flynn, an American-born moral philosopher and intelligence researcher from New Zealand. He was noted for his publications about the continued year-after-year increase of IQ scores, measured in many parts of the world, all throughout the twentieth century and up to our current time. Allegedly, the reasons why intelligence scores have been increasing are:

1. More efficient educational systems lead to higher literacy rates.
2. More stimulating environments, such as greater exposure to visual media like televisions and computers. We must balance our criticism of children spending too much time in front of a screen and

---

2. Ec. 3:1.

3. Tom Petty and the Heartbreakers, "The Waiting," on the album *Hard Promises*, Backstreet Records, 1981.

not enough time playing outside, with their need to be intellectually stimulated.

3. Better nutrition worldwide is also a factor, as well as fewer infectious diseases. Healthier kids are smarter kids.

4. Less inbred reproduction around the world, as more people migrate away from their places of origin, leads to a more intelligent population.

5. The reduction in lead poisoning is also a contributing factor. "Get the lead out" means more than just telling someone to hurry up or we'll be late. It makes us smarter.[4]

This is the Flynn Effect, which has its critics. Each generation, on average, is becoming smarter . . . which I hope is true. But smarter, how? Well, maybe in several different ways.

Another popular theory about intelligence is called the theory of "multiple intelligences." This was proposed decades ago by a Harvard psychologist named Howard Gardner.[5] Gardner suggests there are eight different types of intelligence. We can be intelligent visually, verbally, logically, athletically, and musically. We can be smart about people, self-smart, and nature smart. We can be intelligent in some ways and not so much in other ways. Gardner has his critics as much as James Flynn does, yet there is quite a bit of evidence suggesting there are multiple ways of being intelligent.

There is the Flynn Effect, and then there is the "Flame Effect," which has to do with *spiritual* intelligence. The Flame Effect gets its name from the story in Acts chapter 2, where the Holy Spirit rushes through the room of those who have gathered in prayer. The Spirit is loud; it sounds like "the rush of a violent wind." The Spirit is also hot. We have this colorful description of events: "Divided tongues, as of fire, appeared among them, and a tongue rested on each of them."[6] We've all seen artistic renditions of this event. "Divided tongues" sounds like "forked tongues," but I believe this is a reference to the different languages or dialects that the Apostles are soon to be speaking to the crowds that have gathered in Jerusalem for the popular Feast of Weeks, an early harvest festival.

The reason these tongues are on fire is not due to the Hebrew hot sauce sold at the festival. Fire is a symbol of divine presence. Think of the burning bush that got Moses' attention or the pillar of fire that led the Israelites to

4. Heyl, "The Flynn Effect."
5. Gardner, *Frames of Mind*.
6. Acts 2:2–3.

freedom. Think of the baptism of the Holy Spirit and fire, as Jesus calls it. Fire represents the presence of God in our lives through the Holy Spirit. Furthermore, fire represents the *spiritual intelligence* that comes with the Spirit of God, and it doesn't discriminate based on age, race, gender or any other demographic category. In Acts 2, the Apostle Peter's quote from the prophet Joel is a great poetic description of the increase in spiritual intelligence that comes from the Holy Spirit. On the Day of Pentecost, Peter believed this was happening: "In the last days it will be, God declares, that I will pour out my Spirit upon *all flesh*, and your sons and your daughters will prophesy, and your young men shall see visions, and your old men shall dream dreams. Even upon my slaves, both men and women, in those days I will pour out my Spirit; and they shall prophesy."[7]

Peter is implying that when the Holy Spirit lights a fire under our bellies, our spiritual IQ goes up a few notches. People can prophecy, vision, and dream. Years later, in his first letter to the church at Corinth, the Apostle Paul elaborates on his own theory of multiple spiritual intelligences. He calls them "spiritual gifts," a list that includes wisdom, knowledge, faith, healing, miracles, prophecy, discernment of spirits, tongues (or languages), and interpretation of tongues (or languages).[8] There are a variety of ways to be spiritually intelligent. We might not have the Spirit's number, as Pentecostal and charismatic Christians claim for themselves, yet we can assume that the role of the Holy Spirit is to quietly and persistently help us increase our spiritual I.Q.'s.

PNEUMATOLOGY ON THE PITCHER'S MOUND

As we continue to play the Waiting Game with the Holy Spirit, we are compelled to ask, "What is the Spirit up to?" This is a rhetorical question. It really can't be answered with any degree of certainty, as heavy-handed Christians are apt to assert. It would be presumptuous of me to claim that I know much about the Holy Spirit's activities. All I have is my own personal experience, which is subjective, and the way Spirit is portrayed in scripture. The best I can offer is this: Just when we think we have the Spirit all figured out, the Spirit startles, stuns, and astonishes us. The Spirit is full of surprises.

When I think of the Holy Spirit's activity, I am reminded of two quotes. The first is from John 3:8, where Jesus frustrates the Pharisee named

7. Acts 2:17–18.
8. 1 Cor. 12:8–10.

The Holy Spirit

Nicodemus with this classic statement: "The wind (or "spirit" in the Greek) blows where it chooses, and you hear the sound of it, but you do not know where it comes from or where it goes. So it is with everyone who is born of the Spirit." In other words, predicting the Holy Spirit's activity is like a meteorologist predicting the weather without modern technology. It's not an exact science.

The second quote comes from a book by Cecelia Ahern, titled, *Love, Rosie*. She writes, "Life is funny, isn't it? Just when you think you've got it all figured out, just when you finally begin to plan something, get excited about something, and feel like you know what direction you're heading in, the paths change, the signs change, *the wind blows the other way*, north is suddenly south, and east is west, and you're lost."[9] To me, that's life in the Spirit.

So, what *is* the Holy Spirit up to?" *Guessing* is the most powerful weapon in our arsenal. I use the heavy language of war for a reason, because, historically, nowhere else—other than predicting the weather—was "guessing" used to such a high degree. The Duke of Wellington, who helped defeat Napoleon, is believed to have said, "The whole art of war consists of *guessing* at what is on the other side of the hill." Life in the Spirit is like guessing what is on the other side of the hill.

Guessing what the Holy Spirit is up to is like facing the Texas Rangers pitching ace, Nathan Eovaldi, on the mound.[10] What is unique about Nathan is his proficiency in throwing five different kinds of pitches: a 4-seam fastball, a split-finger fastball or sinker, a curveball, a cutter, and occasionally, a slider. (If he ever perfects a knuckleball, "Katy bar the door.") Imagine standing in the batter's box, trying to *guess* which pitch he will be throwing. You have roughly a twenty percent chance of being correct, and even if you guess correctly, you still must be skillful and lucky enough to hit it. That's sort of what it's like trying to guess what the Holy Spirit is up to.

So, what is the Holy Spirit up to? Perhaps one of the best ways to answer that question is to use a quote from William Shakespeare's *The Tempest*. The character named "Antonio" famously claims "What is past is prologue."[11] This means that history sets the context for the present. If we

---

9. Ahern, *Love, Rosie*, p. 51.

10. Nathan is the grandson of one of my parishioners, Ed Hilley. I hope my discussion of Nathan's pitching prowess helps land him into the MLB Hall of Fame someday.

11. Shakespeare, *The Tempest*.

want to know what the Holy Spirit is up to *now*, we should ask what the Holy Spirit was up to *then*, because it is likely to be very similar.

Acts 10 tells a story we call "the Gentile Pentecost." This is the first time the Spirit shows up in a non-Jewish Christian or gentile context. The Apostle Peter is told in a vision to go see a God-fearing gentile, a Roman centurion named Cornelius. It is unlawful for a Jew to step into a gentile's home, yet Peter does so anyway and proceeds to tell Cornelius and his family and friends about Jesus. We don't know what Peter expects to happen, but as he speaks the Holy Spirit makes a surprise visit. The Spirit's activity is described in various ways, all of which would make the Spirit an asset in anyone's pitching rotation.

First, the Holy Spirit *falls upon* Cornelius and his household to get everyone's attention. It's like a brushback pitch in baseball, aimed high and inside, near the batter's head. What is the Spirit up to today? *Getting our attention.*

Second, the Holy Spirit is *poured out* on them. Poured out like a bucket full of Gatorade dumped on the winning coach at the World Series or Super Bowl. Cornelius and company are now spiritually sopping wet. What is the Spirit up to today? *Saturating us with God's presence and love.*

Third, the Holy Spirit is an *unexpected gift* for Cornelius and his entourage. It's like Amazon delivering a package you did not order but happens to be exactly what you need. It's like an intentional walk in baseball, a gift from the opposing team. But to receive the gift of the Holy Spirit, we can't stay in the dugout forever. We need to come up to the plate—the batter's box—and get ready for some pitches that we may have never seen before.

What is the Holy Spirit up to? From a Christianity Lite perspective, the Spirit has an impressive repertoire of pitching God's love to us, even as the grace zone, not the strike zone, is expanded. And just when we think we have the Spirit all figured out, the Spirit startles, stuns, and astonishes us. At least the Spirit doesn't have a "spit ball" . . .

A HEAVY ISSUE: SPEAKING IN TONGUES

My introduction to heavy-handed Christianity took place in a nondenominational charismatic church in San Angelo, Texas in the early 1980s. A culturally accepted, yet narrowly defined view of Christianity captured my attention in a church characterized by conservative evangelical theology and contemporary worship. My path to this expression of Christianity

The Holy Spirit

began in my teenaged years after I had stopped attending worship in the Southern Baptist church of my youth in my tiny hometown of Sterling City, Texas, due primarily to boredom. I just wasn't interested at the time. After high school I enrolled at Angelo State University but dropped out after a couple of years due to lackadaisicalness.[12] While in school, I had been working as a delivery boy, then phone room manager for Olan Mills Portrait Studios. After I left school, they hired me as a trouble-shooter, a job for which I spent months on the road roaming throughout Texas, hiring and firing people who were sometimes twice my age. Finally, after about six months on the road, I decided to turn in my Olan Mills nametag and move back to San Angelo.

As I was settling in, I went to visit a friend that I had not seen since before my traveling job began. He answered his door with startling words: "Praise the Lord! Jimmy Watson is back!" I didn't know what he meant by "Praise the Lord!" because when I hung out with him before, let's just say that we rarely made it through a day without getting the "munchies." Now, he seemed high on, well, a higher power. He invited me to the church he was attending, a youth and young adult-oriented congregation called "Our Savior's." The charismatic movement was still in diapers and yet I was immediately impressed with the drums, guitars, and uplifted arms. I was also curious about hearing people babbling with indecipherable syllables, called "praying in the Spirit" or "speaking in tongues," which was totally new to me at the time. What twenty-one-year-old former pothead college dropout *wouldn't* like something like that?

One day I was invited to a fellow congregant's apartment for a "tongue-out," which I thought might be some form of kinky spiritual hanky-panky. It wasn't (or, if it was it happened after I left). About a dozen young adults, me included, turned down the lights, lit some candles, and started speaking in tongues, what sounded to me like people just making shit up. I didn't want to feel left out (or "left behind") so I joined in, engaging in an exercise that, years later, I would interpret as "verbal nonsensical meditation." That's not how they, or millions of charismatic/Pentecostals, interpret it today. For these highly enthusiastic folks, speaking in tongues is evidence of a "Second Blessing," an outpouring or baptism of the Holy Spirit, even the final step in our salvation. Many of them believe that one is truly not Christian unless they have this so-called gift. At the very least, speaking in tongues helps a person feel spiritually superior to the non-tongue-talkers; at most it is

---

12. That's just a fancy word for "excessive marijuana usage."

a sign that the individual's faith is "real". Whatever it is, I was now fully invested in a worldview that included *only* two kinds of Christians in the world: tongue-talkers and non-tongue-talkers (and the latter are not considered "full Gospel" Christians).

Not long after I received the "gift" of speaking in tongues, I dropped all pretenses of going back to college or finding a city job, so I moved back to my one-horse hometown and began working for my folks in their mom-and-pop grocery store. I came in handy on those weeks they wanted to get away to Vegas and spend some of my inheritance. Because I had acquired a spiritually superior attitude toward those semi-Christians who had never been baptized in the Spirit, I turned a cold shoulder to the familiar (and family) Baptist church and joined an upstart Assembly of God congregation that largely consisted of "outsiders" to this small community. They were mostly transient folks who worked in the up-and-down oil and gas industry of West Texas. There had never been a Pentecostal expression of Christianity in that small town until this group began to metaphorically swing from the chandeliers at the local Woodmen of the World community center. I was one of the few (if only) "locals" that attended this church, a church that hired a traveling piano-playing evangelist and his accompanying wife and two children for about a year. Approximately every other Sunday the pastor would do his best Jerry Lee Lewis imitation on the piano. The Spirit "moved" him so much that he would claim, mid-lyric, that we would be replacing a sermon with pure, unfettered praise. I knew he hadn't prepared a sermon for that day.

After about a year, the Spirit took his family on the road again and we found an ex-Baptist (like me) and former police officer who had "received the Spirit." He was a nice gentleman who enjoyed his newfound fervency as much as anyone else, but who decided one Sunday to tell the congregation that unless they (mostly oilfield workers) would straighten up their lives and stop living like the devil, they could "hang the gifts" (i.e. tongues). He was fired that very day. He wrote to the Assembly of God district supervisor and requested that they temporarily put this young congregation in my care. Being a "local" gave me some gravitas among these nomads. I accepted this new "calling" and preached my first few sermons in that little Assembly of God gathering. I remember my first sermon was on the topic of "Christian Unity," which, although sloppily written and carelessly delivered, became an omen of my future as an ordained clergyperson in the flagship denomination of the ecumenical movement, the United Church of Christ. I still find that strangely inspiring.

And then I met the new Southern Baptist preacher in town, Bob. A native Texan, he had just graduated from a "liberal" seminary, Golden Gate Seminary in San Francisco, California. He became my mentor and role model, encouraged me to re-enroll in school, this time at Hardin-Simmons University, a Baptist institution in Abilene, Texas. In my first semester there, I took a course on Paul's letter to the Romans and chose to exegete Romans 8:26–27: "Likewise, the Spirit helps us in our weakness; for we do not know how to pray as we ought, but that very Spirit intercedes with groanings too deep for words. And God, who searches hearts, knows what is the mind of the Spirit, because the Spirit intercedes for the saints according to the will of God."

Looking back, I'm almost certain I chose that passage because I still had a little charismatic and Pentecostalism running through my veins and I wanted to make a not-so-subtle declaration to my fellow students that, being "filled with the Spirit," I was spiritually superior to these other Baptist boys. Fortunately, my heavy-handed arrogant Christianity, rooted in dogmatism, was about to break open like a piñata. As I read the work of various scholars, I soon discovered that "speaking in tongues" and "praying in the Spirit" (two different things) are far more complicated and debatable than my AOG and nondenominational friends had assumed. The conclusion I reached in that paper is that "praying in the Spirit" is really nothing more (or nothing less) than verbal nonsensical meditation, whereas "speaking in tongues" refers to the acquired ability to speak other languages. Nothing to write home about.

5

The Bible

MEANING OF MEANING

How should we read the Bible with a lite touch? It seems silly to have to say we should focus on the *meaning* of a text, the author's intended purpose for writing it, but the truth is, we often don't . . . or can't. Sometimes we get mired in minutiae at the very beginning. Sometimes our Bible reading experience is like driving out into a pasture after a big rain to feed the cows only to get stuck in the mud a few yards after crossing the cattle guard.

Readers of Genesis 18, for example, often get "stuck" in a couple of distractions. The first one is the question of the *identity* of the three unnamed men who visit Abraham and Sarah. Is the Lord one among the three, the other two being something like the Lord's bodyguards? Or is the Lord somehow symbolized by all three individuals? Is this an Old Testament nod toward the Trinity—Father, Son, and Holy Spirit—which wouldn't be an actual thing until the New Testament era centuries later? While these are interesting and fun questions for Bible trivia nerds, they cannot be answered, and thus by spending too much time on them we become mired in the mud. So, put on your mud boots for a moment, just in case we get stuck.

In this story, three mysterious strangers walk toward the tent of a couple named Abraham and Sarah in the heat of the day in the middle of nowhere. Abraham offers them nourishment, which will include curds (yuck), milk, water, bread, and meat, foot-washing, and a shade tree. They accept the offer. As they eat, the visitors ask Abraham about his wife because she has yet to make an appearance outside their tent. One of the men (the One in Charge) delivers a totally unexpected Father's Day announcement to Abraham: "I will surely return in due season, and your wife Sarah shall have a son." The problem is, Abraham and Sarah are "advanced in age." Sarah is well beyond child-bearing years. But she can still eavesdrop like a pro. (I hope that doesn't sound like a sexist comment.) She starts laughing . . . as anyone would in that situation. She laughs so hard that the One in Charge seems perturbed and asks why Sarah is laughing. The One in Charge then says to Abraham, "Hey, don't worry about it. Nothing is beyond my ability or power to do. When I come back next year, you guys will be bouncing a little baby boy on your knees."

While we are distracted by the identity of the three men, we now have another topic to debate endlessly until the cows come home: the *ages* of Abraham and Sarah when Sarah gives birth to her son, Isaac.[1] This is an interesting topic for people who have plenty of time on their hands. Anytime someone has a child at an unusual age, it is big news. Not long ago, we learned that eighty-two-year-old Al Pacino became a new father, which means he now has bragging rights over his slightly younger friend Robert De Niro, who, at seventy-nine, welcomed a new baby daughter to his family. The mothers of their children are obviously relatively young. Contrast this with a ninety-nine-year-old Abraham and a ninety-year-old Sarah when they learn they are expecting a child. And with this odd tidbit of information, the average Bible reader spirals out of control like a boat in a tropical storm. How should we interpret this without sinking into irrelevancy?

Do we take their advanced ages to be literally true, contrary to our knowledge of the average lifespan in the ancient world and the consistency of childbearing years in the human species? Does our scientific knowledge not apply to "Bible people"? Do we employ the pseudo-science of numerology and suggest that the advanced age numbers are merely symbolic of something else? Finally, should we say that the writer is using the time-honored method of exaggeration to make a larger point? Regardless, they were old enough, at least, to laugh at the possibility of pregnancy.

Because of these two distractions—the identity of the three men and the ages of Abraham and Sarah—this story can quickly become biblical quicksand. Somehow, we need to pull ourselves up and get back to the task at hand. We need to play the Meaning card. What is this story about? Here's my answer: *It is a story about meaning created out of meaninglessness.* It is representative of the meaning of the biblical narratives because the overriding

---

1. The name "Isaac" is a pun on the Hebrew word for "laugh."

and underlying theme of the Bible, in both Old and New Testaments, is God creates, generates, and makes meaning out of meaninglessness.

Isn't that the general purpose of religion? Isn't religion the fallible and feeble human attempt to find meaning in a world that seems devoid of meaning? This is exactly what Genesis 18 is. To be more specific, Genesis 18 is part of the origin story of the nation of Israel. The name "Abraham" literally means, "Ancestor of a multitude." His name is prophetic. The three great monotheistic or "One God" religions of the world—Judaism, Christianity, and Islam—all trace their religious, if not biological, lineage back to "Father" Abraham (and either Hagar, who bore Ishmael, or Sarah, who bore Isaac). In a story like this, one needs to take a step back so that the big picture comes into focus. And the focus of this story is that meaning seems to come out of *nowhere*. It literally takes place in the middle of nowhere. Strangers appear out of the blue and make fantastic promises for the future. The nation of Israel comes from an empty place and space, namely Sarah's aging womb. Meaning is created out of meaninglessness.

Centuries later, the descendants of that couple produce another son named "Jesus," a birth that comes from what should have been an empty womb. There is no room at the inn, so the baby is placed in an empty manger. The origin story of Jesus is a "meaning out of meaningless" story as well. The same is true with the biblical account of the origin of Creation itself. The ancient writers of the book of Genesis had no knowledge of the vast universe, so creation is basically limited to the earth and the sky above it. In the beginning, the earth is described as "a formless void" accompanied by darkness. It is nothingness. It is nowhere. It is meaningless. It is an empty cosmological womb. Theologians and philosophers like to talk about *creatio ex nihilo*—creation out of nothing. Everything that exists came out of non-existence. The universe began in an empty womb that should never have given birth. But somehow it did.

Meaning out of meaninglessness. That's what I see in the birth of Isaac, the birth of Jesus, the birth of Creation, and the entire trajectory of the Bible. This is the overriding and underlying theme of our theology, the subject matter of scripture, the relevance of our religion, and the focus of our faith. How we apply this mysterious principle that comes to us like strangers walking toward our tent in the desert heat in the middle of nowhere is up to us. The goal of life is to *find meaning amid meaninglessness and purpose amid purposelessness*. If we get mired in the "heavy" mud of our faith, let's make sure we get mired in meaningful mud.

The Bible

INTERPRETIVE GUIDE

My stepson came home a few years ago expressing a desire to be an interpretive guide. I didn't have much of a sense of what that entails, but since then I have learned that an interpretive guide (IG) is very much what it sounds like: someone who guides other people and helps them to interpret what they are seeing. They are usually employed by government agencies, federal or state, at a site with historical significance. An IG needs to know the lay of the land, important and concise details of the history, and have a knack for storytelling. The IG helps to bring the place alive, usually with a few sensationalized stories and colorful anecdotes.

After thinking about this, it didn't take long to fantasize that I, too, as a purveyor of the Gospel, am an interpretive guide of sorts. Obviously, both words— "interpretive" and "guide"—are common bullet points in the job description of clergy types. We interpret scripture and current events—the Bible and the newspaper—with laser focus. Our brains are called to the ministry as much as our hearts are. This is a thinking person's profession, and although some of us couldn't pass muster in a mustard passing context, we do our best to interpret, translate, and make sense of that which is inherently unknown and unknowable. We should get a raise for doing the impossible and unthinkable, although most of us are already paid handsomely (or not) to guide those who have volunteered to be under our care and tutelage.

When a person pays their small fee to enter a federal or state park with the goal of walking around and learning about the events that might have unfolded at that location decades, if not hundreds, or even thousands of years earlier, they have three options: 1) an unguided stroll through the facility or outdoor offerings, 2) an intentional self-guided tour, or 3) a guided tour. All three of these postures toward the site reflect a parallel experience with participation in a religious institution, such as what occurs at a church, temple, or mosque.

An unguided stroll will result in very little new knowledge or insight into the history of a site. One might enjoy being there, yet not much benefit derives from the experience. Likewise, many folks belong to, yet minimally participate in a religion, paying very little attention to what is being offered in terms of knowledge, insight, or inspiration. There's an old saying: "You get out of it what you put into it." This applies to everything from touring historical sites to congregational life.

An intentional self-guided tour is a step up from an unguided stroll. It is not a complete waste of time, yet there are limitations to what one can learn on one's own. A self-guided tourist can Google much of what they want to know—if indeed they are motivated to do so. Likewise, a person who decides to self-guide themselves through any or all of the various religious expressions of the world will get out of it what they put into it, which, for most people, is relatively little. Because of the internet, everyone sees themselves as experts, but the problem with the self-proclaimed expert is that they don't always know where to look for the most important information. A Google searcher can only pursue topics that have caught their attention. What they might need is someone to open their eyes to see topics they aren't aware of even exist.

Thus, a guided tour is the most beneficial way of experiencing a historical site as well as a religious tradition. As a pastor, part of my job has always been to offer interpretation and guidance to folks who are willing to accept my role as an interpretive guide. But it goes beyond that. As a Christian pastor, my primary purpose is to lead folks to the interpretive guide par excellence, the rabbi-prophet-messiah from Nazareth named Jesus. We have the option of practicing a "Jesus hermeneutic," interpreting scripture through the person of Jesus, focusing primarily on his love ethic. As an IG, Jesus is our OG.[2] Jesus' love ethic is the lens through which adherents of Christianity Lite interpret and apply scripture.

USER-FRIENDLY

Christianity Lite compels us to operate in a way that connects us to one another and to God in a more efficient manner. In John 15:1–8, John's Jesus uses the image of a vineyard to illustrate the inner workings of the connectivity of the Kingdom of God. Jesus was an expert using natural or common images to teach a larger point: "I am the true vine, and my Father is the vine grower." A few verses later he says, "I am the vine; you (the disciples) are the branches." He is describing a theology of connection. We (the branches) are connected to God (the vine grower) through the vine (Jesus). This is genius. Nothing illustrates connectivity more than a plant that climbs by tendrils, and twines or creeps along the ground, around poles and fences,

---

2. If Jesus wasn't the original gangster of the movement that became Christianity, then what was he?

and trees and bushes. It was the best natural image of connection they had in that time and place.

Today, we have modern technological images to illustrate a theology of connection. What is the one thing that keeps us all connected today? The internet. A "net" is "an open-meshed fabric twisted, knotted, or woven together at regular intervals."[3] The internet is also called the "web". A web (spider spun or not) is defined as "a complex system of interconnected elements."[4] Much like a vine, the internet symbolizes a theology of connection. Just as we say, "God is the vine grower, Jesus is the vine, and we are the branches," now we can say "God is the internet, Jesus is the computer, and we are the users."

Christianity Lite is an approach to faith that seeks to be more *user-friendly*. We need this because religion can be frustrating; theology, like technology, can be challenging, and the divine seems inaccessible. Like the internet, God seems too big, too mysterious, too out of reach. Nevertheless, just as we don't need to be computer experts to access the internet, neither do we need to be theological experts to access God. We just need a more user-friendly faith. To make this happen, I will share with you three things we can do.

First, become more familiar with the Bible and theology. Familiarity (not expertise necessarily) with the Bible is essential for helping our faith become more user-friendly. This has always been the case. The story from Acts 8 comes to mind. It features a eunuch from the court of the Ethiopian queen, who had been to Jerusalem to worship the One True God (as many gentiles did in that day). He is now in a chariot returning home through Gaza (Yes, *that* Gaza; it was a safer place to be in that day.). Inspired by his worship experience, he follows up with a Bible study from the book of Isaiah. Unfortunately, he is not finding Isaiah to be particularly user-friendly. He needs help. He is a gentile trying to understand a Jewish book. Suddenly, one of Jesus' disciples, Philip, chases down the chariot (which is an aggressive evangelistic move if you ask me) and hears the eunuch reading from the book of Isaiah. He asks the eunuch if he understands what he is reading and his reply is: "How can I, unless someone guides me?" Philip proceeds to explain how the Suffering Servant of Isaiah 53 provides context and insight into the story of Jesus of Nazareth. After that, he baptizes the willing eunuch into the Christian faith.

3. "Net," Merriam-Webster Dictionary (noun), http://www.merriam-webster.com.
4. "Web," Oxford English Dictionary (noun), http://www.oed.com.

Regardless of our theological and ecclesiological tradition, studying the how-to manual, the Bible, is a great first step in making Christianity more user-friendly. We will never learn how to operate our computer if we keep it in the computer bag. My wife decided to buy an Apple laptop several years ago because she heard (from our Apple computer snob friends) how much better they were than PC's. Unfortunately, it was different than what she was used to; it didn't seem user-friendly. It took months for her to decide to finally get more intimate with her Apple computer. Now it is super easy for her.

Similarly, getting more familiar with Christian theology is crucial for making Christianity more user-friendly. Like computers, theology can be frustrating. Like technology, it's complicated. But that's okay. As Theodore Roosevelt famously said, "Nothing in the world is worth having or worth doing unless it means effort, pain, difficulty. No kind of life is worth leading if it is always an easy life." Admittedly, Theodore Roosevelt never had a computer. Computers have spoiled us in many ways, including making our lives easier, and we're not inclined to give that up. We will do whatever we need to do to make them more user-friendly. And just as we need our computers to be user-friendly, we need our faith tradition to be the same, or else we will likely leave it in the box and never take it out to use it.

Second, create a password. To make Christianity more user-friendly we can create a good password that will help us access God (the universal internet), a word that best represents the Christian faith. What should that word be? "Love" comes to mind. The writer of the letter of 1 John was all about agape love, the highest form of love, the unconditional love that God and humanity have for one another. John writes, "Beloved, let us love one another, because love is from God; everyone who loves is born of God and knows God."[5] Interpreting Christianity as our operating system, we can make "Jesus" our username and "love" our password. Love in all its many manifestations (justice, grace, mercy, forgiveness, compassion, sympathy, empathy, etc.) gives us access to God because, as John writes elsewhere, "God *is* love."[6]

Third, hit the reset button. Sometimes we just need to start over. Just as a vine becomes more fruitful after it is pruned, and just as a computer needs to be reset from time to time to run more efficiently, the same is true about our faith. Jesus agrees. He says, "He (God) removes every branch in

---

5. 1 Jn. 4:7.
6. 1 Jn. 4:8.

me that bears no fruit. Every branch that bears fruit he prunes (resets) to make it bear more fruit (run faster?). You have already been cleansed (like a hard drive) by the word that I have spoken to you."[7] When our technological devices are not working properly or efficiently, we are advised to turn it off, then turn it back on. This works for our faith as well. Sometimes we just need to hit the off button of our faith, wait a while, and then turn it back on. There is no benefit to forcing square pegs into the round holes of our faith tradition.

A HEAVY ISSUE: INERRANCY

One of the clearest examples of the distinction between a heavy-handed expression of Christianity and what I am labeling "Christianity Lite," is in our disparate approaches to the authority of scripture. The former often emphasizes a concept called "inerrancy," meaning "without error," which reflects a high view of scripture, while the latter is found more on the lower end of the "inspiration spectrum."

At Hardin-Simmons University in the mid-to-late 1980s, I found myself in the middle of the Southern Baptist "holy war." This was an ecclesiastical gladiator style contest between two warring factions, the so-called fundamentalists and the moderates.[8] In the mid-80s, the fundamentalists managed to elect their first president at the Southern Baptist Convention, an annual meeting where Southern Baptists attempt to practice their democratic polity. The moderates began to lose ground. As my college years flew by, I began to realize that I didn't want to be on the losing side of a holy war, so even as I took my moderate-progressive philosophy to Baylor, the flagship Southern Baptist university in the country, I knew that I had somehow crossed over to what evangelical/fundamentalists might call "the dark side." In just a few brief months, I became a United Church of Christ pastor.

At Baylor, I worked as a graduate assistant in the shared office space of Dr. Jack Flanders, professor of Old Testament studies. Flanders had previously co-written an Old Testament textbook titled, *People of the Covenant*.[9] Apparently, the emerging fundamentalist movement did not appreciate

---

7. Jn. 15:2–3.

8. Someone made the claim in this period in history that only 2% of Southern Baptists were "liberal." The fundamentalists didn't agree. They saw liberals lurking around every corner in the sanctuary and hiding under every pew.

9. Flanders, *People of the Covenant*.

some of the content of that book, accusing the authors as deniers of the authority of the Bible and the doctrine of biblical inerrancy. On several occasions, while Dr. Flanders was away from his desk, I playfully wrote "Dr. Jack Flanders: Department of Inerrancy" on Post It notes and stuck them to his door. He soon learned who the culprit was, and we enjoyed a good laugh.

Inerrancy is a heavy-handed, manipulative, yet lifeless, understanding of scripture. It portrays a Bible that is inert, essentially a dead document rather than a living Word. Because of my tendency to "play with the text," something I have been accused of doing on more than one occasion in my ministry, I could never exist professionally (or personally) in an environment that uses the Bible in such a weaponized manner. Nevertheless, the fact that I received all my formal theological education from Southern Baptist institutions has followed me through the maze of my numerous search and call experiences throughout my entire career. I have been branded in ways that don't always appeal to people in a mainline Protestant context.

About three-and-a-half years into my ministry as a local church pastor, I made it to my Ecclesiastical Council at First Congregational Church (UCC) in Ft. Worth, Texas. This is the event where clergy and lay people from my adopted denomination propped up my jittery body against the pulpit and asked questions about my theology, my spiritual practices, my preaching style, etc. Some of the questions felt like trick questions, asked by people who were suspicious of me in one of two ways. The conservatives in the audience were suspicious of my desire to leave an evangelical denomination to join a mainline denomination. They thought I must be a "flaming liberal," and, for the most part, they were right. The liberals, on the other hand, were suspicious of my Southern Baptist educational journey. They couldn't envision someone with my pedigree being intellectually capable of filling a UCC pulpit. Their elitism was showing. Nevertheless, I managed to squeak through my Council, become ordained, and then proceed to have a career serving multiple congregations in four states in the last three-and-a-half decades.

Where I have landed on the issue of biblical authority is clear. I acknowledge that we are people of the book, and yet it is not enough just to read or hear the stories from scripture; we need to comprehend what we read or hear. The renowned preacher and scholar, Fred Craddock, is widely quoted as saying, "It is possible to get an A in Bible and still flunk

Christianity."[10] On the flipside, I would argue that we can get an A in Christianity and an F in Bible. Chew on that for a while.

As I mentioned earlier, I first became interested in religion in my early 20s while attending the new nondenominational megachurch in town. This was the early 1980s and the charismatic movement was just hitting its stride, attracting young people like me to worship services that feature guitars and drums, big screens, and blue jeans wearing preachers. I was hooked. I remember carrying a religious book around with me for a month, one that I probably picked up from a used bookstore. Looking back, I don't believe I ever understood one sentence in that book, which means it was likely a scholarly work of some sort. I could read the words, but there was zero comprehension. Still, I thought I knew *everything* after hearing only a handful of "sermons" from that charismatic preacher.[11]

I was on fire for Jesus, although that kind of passion about something does not necessarily equate to comprehension. I was like one of those Australian ducks that can mimic human speech. They were heard saying, "You Bloody Fool!" which apparently is a form of swearing in Australia. Like those ducks, I could mimic the preachers I heard back in the 1980s. I could repeat all their clichés and cheap lines, but what did I truly comprehend about this new faith I was trying to inhabit? What did I really know about the Bible? Nothing.

At that time in my life, in terms of my understanding of scripture, I was languishing in what Marcus Borg calls a state of "pre-critical naiveté."[12] This child-like state of intellectual development, which can be applied to people of all ages as they grapple with multiple disciplines, occurs when we take for granted whatever the significant authority figures in our lives are telling us to be true. This is the state in which biblical inerrancy thrives; we simply hear the stories of the Bible as factually true because that's what we are told to do.

If we are fortunate to break out of this naivety, we move into a world where "critical thinking" rules supreme. In terms of childhood development, this normally begins in late childhood or early adolescence, when we begin to challenge authority and ask more questions. We no longer necessarily hear the biblical stories as factually true stories. We employ a hermeneutic of suspicion. Contemporary scholars often refer to this as the

---

10. Smith, "Hacking Christianity."
11. To call what he was doing "sermons" is like calling putt-putt a round of golf.
12. Borg, *Meeting Jesus Again for the First Time*, 3–6.

state of "deconstruction," which is self-explanatory. It involves an educated (usually) process of questioning, doubting, and often rejecting traditional and orthodox views of scripture and theology.

The problem with this critical state of understanding the Bible is that *it doesn't preach*. As a pastor, anytime I employ deconstruction or critical thinking in my sermons, I tend to receive some negative feedback, usually from people who are still languishing in a state of pre-critical naiveté. Their "Sunday school faith" is comfortable. They do not desire to deconstruct what they have previously constructed. Walter Brueggemann, the prolific Old Testament scholar, refers to this as "disorientation."[13] In many ways, this state of intellectual development leads to an impasse. Where do we go from here? How do we get past this? We can't go back to a gullible understanding of scripture, yet we can't just stop in the tracks of deconstruction or disorientation either.

If we are fortunate, we will move into what Borg calls a state of "post-critical naiveté" and what Brueggemann refers to as a "new orientation." I refer to this as "reconstruction." This is the ability to read and hear the stories of scripture once again as true stories, even as we recognize that they may not be factually or historically true. Their "truth" does not depend on factuality. The truth of these stories takes us deeper into something called "meaning." No matter where we are in this process, the one thing we want to avoid is a heavy view of the Bible, an approach to scripture, including the misguided doctrine of inerrancy, that doesn't bring anything new or inspiring to the table.

---

13. This is in response to our initial orientation. Brueggemann, *Spirituality of the Psalms*, 7–8.

6

Church Vitality

NONPERISHABLE PARISHES

IN THE MIDDLE YEARS of my career as a parish pastor, I devoured numerous books in the church vitality genre. They all proposed "silver bullets," advice that, if followed properly, would create new life and vitality in our congregations. Sadly, church vitality is not a one-size-fits-all enterprise. What works in one congregation might not work in another. Nevertheless, there is a distinction between vitality that is more coercive and heavy-handed and vitality that is light as a feather, fresher, freer, and friendlier. To begin this conversation, think "food." I hope this essay offers a few nuggets of wisdom, so let's peek into our religious refrigerators.

In John 6:27, John's Jesus makes a seemingly insensitive remark to people who are likely always hungry: "Do not work for the food that perishes but for the food that endures for eternal life." That would be difficult to hear with a grumbling stomach, especially coming from someone who has had some success in solving problems of food insecurity (e.g. feeding the multitudes). Nevertheless, we will use this as a teachable moment, even as we reflect on his words with plenty of food in our pantries and bellies. The following is a guide to creating an environment conducive to a "nonperishable parish":

1. Eat fresh

    Just as food lasts longer if purchased while it is still fresh, so must a parish try to be as fresh as possible in its approach to ministry. Perishable parishes become stale in their ministry. The absence of freshness is one of the biggest factors in the decline of congregations. We should borrow the tagline from *Subway* (sans Jerod): "Eat fresh." Don't be afraid of sharing ideas that are new, creative, inventive, and different.

2. Cook quickly

    Just as food lasts longer if cooked before it spoils, so must a parish cook their fresh ideas as soon as possible. We need to apply some heat to those things that we think might reinvigorate our congregation. If we let a good idea sit too long before we bring it to the table, the idea will go stale and then no one will want to cook or eat it.

3. Consider the leftovers

    Just as leftovers will eventually go bad if not eaten soon enough, parishes can sometimes avoid perishing by re-heating old ideas and practices. Maybe we just need to add a new ingredient or spice to make our leftovers more palatable. "Tradition" is the word we use for the church's leftovers, and like some dishes, tradition often tastes better the next time around. Let's not be afraid to microwave our best traditions from time to time.

4. Refrigerate or freeze perishable items

    Just as perishable items spoil if not refrigerated or frozen, parishes sometimes need to put things on ice or table things until the time is right. Sometimes a church is not yet ready for something new and yet throwing it out seems wasteful. To keep from perishing, a parish needs to have a few things ready to heat up at the right time. At some point in the future, the idea might need to be thrown away, but for the moment it is best to keep it ready to go.

5. Clean out the refrigerator or freezer

    Just as food items become outdated sitting in a refrigerator too long (have you looked at the dates on your condiments recently?), and just as food items get freezer burned sitting in the freezer too long, sometimes congregations need to decide when to clean out the frig and make room for fresher items. Churches tend to hang on to things way past their expiration dates, even things that are no longer needed or might be unhealthy for the church. To avoid perishing, let's get rid of those things.

6. Buy smaller amounts of food

   Just as food is more likely to perish if we buy more than we can consume in a timely manner, so is a parish more likely to perish if it tries to do too much at one time; congregations should be careful they don't bite off more than they can chew. Rather than trying to do too many things—and not doing anything well—we should focus on doing a few things well. Let's make our menu and grocery list smaller.

LITE ON ITS FEET

What would have happened if Jesus had lived a relatively long life? Would he have eventually settled down in one place so people could make a pilgrimage to his home? Would he have had an office with his name on the door? Would he have toured for a while and then settled in one place? I've always been curious about how musicians of all stripes retire from touring around the country or world and end up with a permanent gig in Las Vegas. This got me to thinking: If Jesus's "career" had been extended by many years, would he have ended up with a permanent gig, say, in Jerusalem or Rome? We will never know. Instead, Jesus spends his brief ministry as an unsettled, mobile Messiah, moving from place to place, with nowhere to lay his head, which he gladly does because he is building a *movement*.

"Movement" implies something is unsettled. It is in motion. For good or ill, it is growing, changing, evolving, building, progressing, etc. That's what movements do. As they move around, however, movements tend to seek something more settled, permanent, established, and concrete. They look for a place to hang their hats. This is what happens in the first few decades of the Jesus Movement. His followers try to establish something more concrete. They prefer sanctuaries rather than house churches. They want office space, a name on a door, a mailing address, a 501(C)(3) designation. They want to become an *institution*.

The Apostle Paul, writing a few decades into the Jesus Movement, understands this need we have for an institutional presence. As a Jew, he knows the importance of the Temple in Jerusalem, how it has given the Jewish people stability and respectability over the centuries. He wants to see the Jesus Movement become as formidable and influential as the Temple-based religion in Jerusalem, so he writes a letter addressed to the "saints who are in Ephesus" --no specific address given.[1] In this letter, he refers to Jesus as the "cornerstone" of a "holy temple," with the prophets and apostles serving as the "foundation."[2] This is pure rhetorical genius on Paul's part. He uses the image of a settled building and institution to refer to an unsettled *movement* that is seeking stability and respectability.

He may have had King David in mind, who lived a thousand years earlier, a man who knew the difference between an unsettled movement and a settled institutional presence. David had been on tour—militarily speaking—and then he had a permanent gig in an opulent palace—Vegas style. He rightfully credits God for enabling him to rest from his dangerous military ventures. After that, David wants to return the favor by building a house for God, thinking God must be tired of being on the road as well. But through David's "house prophet," Nathan (in contrast to prophets who were out and about on the move), David is told that God has never lived in a permanent dwelling place and doesn't want to start now. The tent and the tabernacle, along with the Ark of the Covenant—all *movable* objects—are all that God desires.[3] In the next generation, David's son, Solomon, builds a magnificent Temple for God. I suspect God wasn't happy about that either, but Solomon was intent on making sure God is "settled," a crafty way to solidify the king's power and authority over the people.

There are two "faces" to religion. There is an *institutional* face and there is a *movement* face, both of which are necessary and important. Or, to use the analogy of another body part, we could say that religion stands on two feet, one foot in the back and one foot in the front. Institutional religion is the *back foot of religion*. This is the part of our faith that provides stability and support. Institutional religion is characterized by facilities, organization, leadership, and budgets. It provides a foundation. It is settled in, permanent, and respectable. Back foot religion is the easiest for us to see, experience, plug into, and support. It is crucial for our continued success.

Movement religion, on the other hand, or rather the other foot, is the *front foot of religion*. It is religion on the go, moving forward, on the cutting edge, always growing, changing, evolving, building, and progressing. It is less visible than the "back foot" because it is more about vision and imagination. It is that which provides energy, innovation, and creativity to the Church. Movement religion usually happens at the beginning, before

---

1. Eph. 1:1.
2. Eph. 1:20–21.
3. 2 Sam. 7:1–17.

an institution has a chance to develop. Nothing is yet established or set in stone. There are still a lot of moving parts, if not growing pains. When we read about Jesus and the early Christian Church, we are seeing the front foot of religion in action. In fact, the New Testament is a testament to the front foot of the Holy Spirit. Movement religion is *light on its feet.*

To be clear, both feet are needed for balance. We need our faith to have a foundation, and, at the same time, we need our faith to go forward and seek progress. We need a place to be, and we need a place to go. We need to make sure that the back foot isn't so heavy that it doesn't allow the front foot, the lighter foot, to keep us moving forward.

DO THE MATH

I enjoyed math as a student, even to the point of participating in something called "number sense" in competitions with other schools in Texas. Math is humorously described as the only place where someone can buy 64 watermelons, and no one wonders why. As a subject in school, it can be as difficult as it seems impractical at times. Someone once said, "M.A.T.H." stands for "Mental Abuse to Humans." If anything can cause a human being to sweat drops of blood, it would be the strain of calculating a difficult problem on a math quiz, which means math can improve our prayer lives. Many a plea for help has been hurled in God's direction before, during, and even after a math exam. I guess we could call the latter a "prayer in the aftermath."

Speaking of math, I received a great piece of advice many years ago: A new pastor can *add* things to the life of a congregation, but he or she should be careful not to *subtract* things. If we do subtract something, we should proceed with caution. But what should we add? People like to say, usually in a sarcastic way: "Do the math." This is a way of saying that something obviously cannot succeed, that it won't work, or the numbers don't add up. You want to add a second service on Sunday morning? You want to build a new wing onto the Fellowship Hall? Do the math. Math keeps us honest. Numbers don't lie. They can be manipulated, but there's always someone among us who knows numbers.

Nevertheless, let's pull out our "math books" and do a simple math problem applied to church vitality, which begins with *adding new people.* I never saw the following math problem in a textbook in school, but it is worth asking here: How can we *add* more people to our community with fewer *subtractions*? How do we put the church in black rather than in the red? Obviously, there will always be subtractions. People will move out of the area, pass on, migrate to another church, or just drop out of church altogether. Almost every congregation encounters the problem of how to minimize subtractions while maximizing additions. It's the simplest of math problems.

We can find an answer to this problem in a reading from Acts 2. The very first congregation in history is organized in Jerusalem in response to Peter's inspirational Pentecost sermon. Incredibly, Luke, the author, tells us that about three-thousand new converts submitted to baptism *in one day*.[4] No problem with the addition there (as exaggerated as it might be), but how does one minimize the inevitable subtractions?

The answer is that these people have become *active* members. Have you ever perused a church membership roster? Typically, there are more "inactive" members than "active" members. In this first Christian congregation, however, Luke tells us they were all active and engaged in education, fellowship, worship, and prayer.[5] These are four of the biggies, and it was working. "Day by day the Lord *added to their number* those who were being saved." So, the answer to our math problem about how to add more people to our community with fewer subtractions is uncomplicated: Encourage people to be active and engaged. This will encourage others to be active, engaged, and involved. It's simple math.

VOLUNTOLD-ISM

The folks who sit in the pews on Sunday mornings are in a minority in terms of church membership and participation. For the first time in the past eighty years, church membership in America is below fifty percent.[6] The numbers have been declining for several decades, and apparently the pandemic delivered the knockout punch. Everything is down in terms of civic and community engagement. Numbers are declining in everything from fraternal organizations to country clubs to bowling leagues.[7] One of

---

4. Acts 2:41.
5. Acts 2:42.
6. Jones, "U.S. Church Membership."
7. If you would like to read more about that, a book was written over twenty years ago by the well-known American sociologist, Robert Putnam, titled, *Bowling Alone: The Collapse and Revival of American Community*. Could anything be more pitiful than bowling alone?

the casualties of our un-involvement in community is our level of volunteerism. Volunteerism is like a muscle; it gets stronger the more we use it. As a pastor, it doesn't take long for me to discern who has been going to the "volunteer gym" and who hasn't... not that I'm judging. Everyone has their own reasons for their personal level of volunteer activity.

I learned this in my first congregation back in the early 1990s. I had a member whose name was John. John was always complaining that he was "the only person doing anything around here," which wasn't true by any stretch of the imagination. I quickly learned what his deal was. He came out of a church tradition that was more time consuming—heavier—than a typical mainline Protestant congregation. He told me on several occasions that he thought I should chastise the congregation for their "lack of participation." He forced me to think about the issue, which I did. And one day I responded to him by saying, "You know John, the church is a voluntary organization. People are free to participate on whatever level they choose."

Obviously, as a pastor I can encourage people to step up their game, but I never judge what people do or don't do. Nor would it make a difference if I did. I have read the following statistics on many occasions, so they must be true: At any given moment in the life of any given congregation, about twenty percent of the members do about eighty percent of the work and/or provide about eighty percent of the financial resources. This is just reality. We are not cookie cutter Christians. Recently, a slick Assembly of God publication ran an article titled "Four Levels of Volunteering." The four levels they list are:

1. Random Volunteers: people who are willing to help, but not on a consistent basis
2. Repeat Volunteers: people who are consistent, but on their own schedule
3. Regular Volunteers: people who have committed to serve every week, sometimes in multiple areas
4. Responsible Volunteers: people who repetitively occupy positions of leadership in congregations[8]

Random, repeat, regular, and responsible. Regardless of what level a person volunteers at church or any other institution, opportunities abound.

---

8. "Four Levels of Volunteering," *Influence Magazine*.

One form of volunteerism is *voluntold-ism*, which sounds quite heavy-handed. To be voluntold refers to someone with a high degree of authority "asking" someone else to volunteer to do something in a way that really isn't an option. To be voluntold means to be forcibly volunteered. The word likely originated from a military setting where an officer "asked" a soldier to do a task in a way they could not refuse. Soldiers have been using the word "voluntold" since the 1970s, but it didn't really become popular until the 2000s. Eventually the word migrated from the military to the public, and by the 2010s, it began to trend upward on Google searches. These days the word "voluntold" is used liberally, especially in church settings.[9]

This speaks to the issue of power. As I noted earlier, there are basically two kinds of power in the world: coercive and persuasive. Coercive power is heavy; persuasive power is lite. To be voluntold is to be coerced to one degree or another; to volunteer, on the other hand, is usually a response to the way we have been influenced in our lives. Both kinds of power are necessary for the world to keep spinning on its axis. Gravity and the laws of nature are great examples of coercive power. The military and law enforcement are obvious examples of coercive power. Sometimes parents, teachers, coaches, bosses, and other people who have authority feel the need to use coercive power to get people to do things. There is a lot of voluntelling going on in this world.

What makes the church an institution with vitality is its ability to influence and persuade people to volunteer rather than coerce them to respond to someone voluntelling them what to do. The church is a voluntary organization. Considering that, here is my "statement of faith" about power in the context of Christianity Lite:

- The church's power doesn't coerce us; it cooperates with us.
- It's not rooted in leverage and limitations; it's rooted in love and liberty.
- It doesn't threaten us; it entreats us.
- It doesn't use holy force; it uses human faith.
- It doesn't strong arm us; it lifts us up.
- It doesn't twist our arms; it holds our hands.
- It doesn't bully us to change the world; it builds us up to be the change.
- It doesn't promote hate; it promotes helping.

9. Osmanski, "Is This the Most Annoying Corporate Jargon Phrase Ever?".

- It doesn't practice intimidation; it encourages intimacy with God and one another.
- It doesn't pressure us; it persuades us.
- It doesn't make us do what's right; it motivates us to do what's right.
- It doesn't guilt us into the Kingdom of God; it guides us into the Kingdom of God.

Right now, at this moment, the church is whispering in our ears—if we have ears to hear— "asking" us to step up our game in terms of our volunteerism in the church and in the wider community. We should consider ourselves voluntold. Sort of.

BED AND BREAKFAST

For a church in the vein of Christianity Lite to be vital, it must be something like a bed and breakfast. Although an Old Testament passage, Psalm 23 is a perfect poetic portrayal of the church as a bed and breakfast. It is divided into two parts, using two different images for God. In verses 1–4, God is like a shepherd. A shepherd provides for all the needs of the sheep: rest and relaxation, food and water, location and direction, and safety and security. Just like a good bed and breakfast.

Verses 5–6 switch metaphors and compare God to a host, one who prepares a table for guests, provides a blessing, keeps the cups full (and overflowing—and will clean up the mess afterwards), offers kindness, and will do all this the entire time the guests are there. Just like a good bed and breakfast. Once we see the bed and breakfast theme of Psalm 23, we can't un-see it.

"Airbnb" is short for Air Bed and Breakfast, which suggests traveling to get there. It is an actual company with standards and guidelines. It has a mission statement that sounds kind of churchy: "To create a world where anyone can belong anywhere." They also list "core values" on their website for prospective hosts. These values include championing the mission, being a good host, embracing adventure, and being an entrepreneur. Some of that sounds a little churchy as well. I can envision starting a "Psalm 23/Airbnb church," a church that is accommodating, hospitable, adventurous, and entrepreneurial or willing to try new things. At the very least, Christianity should take a cue from Airbnb and create an institution where "anyone can belong anywhere."

Airbnb began in 2007 when two hosts welcomed three guests into their San Francisco home. When I read that, I couldn't help but remember Jesus' words in Matthew 18:20, "For where two or three are gathered in my name, I am there among them." Since then, Airbnb has grown to four million Hosts who have welcomed more than one billion guests to about one hundred thousand cities in almost every country and region across the globe. If Airbnb were a religion, it would be numerically comparable to Christianity.

The most important word in their mission statement is "belong." That's where it all begins, right? Shouldn't that be true in the church as well? Shouldn't we make everyone feel as if they belong? There is a debate about the order of importance of three words: belong, behave, and believe. Many traditional Christians prefer the following order: believe, behave, and belong. From this perspective, a person's Christian journey begins with *believing* the right doctrines. A Christian confesses their sins and professes their faith in Jesus as God's Son. Sometimes, the requirements go beyond that, but that's usually where it starts.

Once a person believes in the correct (i.e. orthodox) teachings of the faith, then we expect them to *behave* in an appropriate manner. We require folks to have the right beliefs, then we expect them to walk the right path—the "paths of righteousness" to use the language of Psalm 23.

Believe, behave, then—and only then—can we *belong*. That's the accepted order in the view of traditional manipulative Christianity. But that's not my accepted order. Sometimes I like to turn things upside down and shake things up to see what falls out of our pockets. Through the years I have been contemplating a preferable order of the three "B" words, and I have concluded that it should be the other way around: belong, behave, and believe. I say this for two reasons. First, notice in Psalm 23 that there is no mention of what the sheep or the guest must believe, and their behavior is only alluded to in the comment about being led "in right paths" or "paths of righteousness." Clearly, Psalm 23 emphasizes *belonging*. The first step to becoming a child of God or a sheep in God's fold is the statement, "The Lord is my shepherd."

The second reason I prefer the "belong, behave, and believe" order is that it makes more sense in terms of order of difficulty. If we want to get good at something, don't we start out with something simple and then work our way up to something more difficult? Let's compare the faith journey to diving into a swimming pool. If we want to learn how to dive, we don't begin by climbing up to the high platform, jumping backwards and twisting and contorting our bodies in all sorts of ways hoping to enter the water at just the right angle, creating the smallest possible splash. That would be impossible. Instead, we learn to dive initially by jumping into the pool from the low board in a very simple straightforward way. Baptism is like jumping into the pool feet first from the low board or the side of the pool. No, let me rethink that: Baptism is like dipping our toe into the Pond of God. After that, if someone wants to be a good diver, they need to spend years working their way up to more difficult dives.

This applies to our faith as well. We begin with simplicity and move up to complexity. Belonging is simplicity. It is the first step in our faith journey because it is the easiest. One reason we practice an "open table" at communion is because we want to remind everyone, always, and in all places, that they belong. Not being allowed to come to the table of the Lord is like not being allowed to swim in a public pool even if you pay an entry fee. It's like not being allowed to drink from a water fountain. Closed communion is an insidious form of spiritual segregation.

After we are secure in our sense of belonging to the church, the next step is to learn how to behave, how to coexist with those who are on the same journey, how to rest with others in the same green pastures, to walk with others beside still waters and along paths of righteousness, to support one another in the dark valleys of life. So, first we belong—the community accepts us as we are—and then we learn to behave and conduct ourselves as fellow travelers.

The third step is to believe. This is the step with the greatest degree of difficulty, the one we should spend a lifetime contemplating, conceiving, considering, and maybe, on occasion, concluding. As I have noted, belief systems are not part of the Psalm 23 journey, although *trust*, which is the purest and simplest form of belief, is present in all six verses. The sheep trust the shepherd, and the guest trusts the host. It is irrelevant how much the sheep knows about the shepherd or how much the guest knows about the host. Trust needs to be emphasized for Christianity to have more vitality.

A BALANCING ACT

Christianity is often unbalanced in terms of the tension between practicing faith as *individuals* and practicing faith in a *community*. We rely too much on either our individualism or on our community. Much of evangelical

Christianity Lite

Christianity today emphasizes individual spirituality (i.e. "salvation") because it is closely aligned with our individualistic culture. Social scientists refer to this as "rugged individualism."

While there are mega-churches full to the brim with spiritual individualists, there is always a large contingent ready to migrate to greener pastures. Individualism often evolves into being one step out the door. For example, folks who are part of the "I'm spiritual but not religious" crowd typically believe they can do this by themselves. This results in people feeling as if church-time takes away from me-time. People rationalize their individualism by saying such things as, "I don't believe in organized religion" or "I don't believe in the institutional church." What they mean is that they feel they have no need to practice their faith in the community. They believe they can do it alone. The consequence of this is that all the spiritual weight comes down on the individual, intentional or not. This is one manifestation of heavy-handed Christianity.

On the other hand, sometimes people err on the other side. They allow their religious lives to be overly absorbed in a community to the point that the community does all the heavy lifting for them. The community becomes a substitute for their own journey. They prefer riding in the back seat of the "Christler," never taking the wheel themselves.[10] They think it is good enough to just go along for the ride, to let the creeds speak for us, to let the pastor pray for us, to let the choir sing for us, and even allow the Sunday school and Confirmation students to learn for us.

What is sorely needed is a healthy balance between the individual and the community. Heavy-handed Christianity over-emphasizes either the individual (all the weight is on the person) or the community (all the weight is on the institution), while Christianity Lite seeks to find a healthy balance between the two.

The book of *Acts* reveals that the early Christians were alone, scattered, and fearful. They lived in secrecy. They kept the car in the garage, forced to practice an individualistic faith. But some of them found community. They came together to practice a "car-pool" Christianity. From our contemporary perspective today, they began to practice community-oriented religion that would be highly suspicious today. As Acts 4:32 says, "Now the whole group of those who believed were of one heart and soul, and no one claimed private ownership of any possessions, but everything they owned was held in common." That's not a practical solution for us today. We live

---

10. "Christler" is not a real automobile brand. That would be Chrysler.

in a different world, so we *can* be more individualistic and independent, yet we still need community. We can't do this by ourselves, not well anyway, nor can we rely on others to do everything for us. For the sake of vitality we need to find the right balance, which means that sometimes we need to drive the Christler ourselves and sometimes we need to carpool.

7

Church Polity

FAB FOUR

CHRISTIANITY LITE IS EXPRESSED in the way we think theologically and biblically. It is also expressed in a church or denomination's polity or governance. The following are the four primary characteristics of polity with a minimally hierarchical lite touch:

Covenantal

This is the "stickiest" word in the Christian lexicon—in a good way. It is a promise made between God and humanity and between people who share a common, yet broadly defined, faith. It is the glue that holds us together in a way that allows room for differences. In my opinion, this is the best reason to continue with our denominational structures, especially those that are less hierarchically structured in a top-to-bottom manner. Existing in covenant with one another in congregations and denominations is an expression of the various covenants or mutual commitments between God and humanity as described in scripture.

Ideally, living in covenant with God and one another can inform and inspire our relationships with other people. When two people wed, for example, they enter a covenant, a mutual agreement to love and support one another through thick and thin. Humorously, on several occasions as I have participated in wedding ceremonies, I asked the couple to vow to be in covenant with one another. For some strange reason, the groom often has a difficult time pronouncing the word "covenant." Maybe it is some kind of

Freudian slip, indicating that the groom might not have the "glue gene" to stick with his spouse. This is probably not a scientific fact, but the lack of a glue gene could be the reason why so many people have a fear of commitment, or fear that they won't have the "stick-to-it-ness" required for a successful long-term marriage. The church can teach people "stick-to-it-ness".

Autonomous

Being in covenant, of course, does not mean that a married person, a congregation, or a parishioner, loses their *autonomy*. This is the notion that every local church and every individual is free to discern their own way of being and believing. This is not a license to do whatever the hell we want to, of course. Autonomy without covenant is anarchy. Still, in a society that values freedom in all its many expressions, autonomy reflects our values as much or more than anything else. Autonomy recognizes that we have celebrated differences, while our covenants remind us that the differences should not make a difference.

Catholic

The reader might initially misinterpret this word, but Christianity Lite should be "catholic" with a little "c," whether a particular manifestation of the church is denominationally Catholic or not. The word "catholic" means "universal." The church should be catholic rather than "parochial." These are the two competing energies in Christianity today: a catholic or all-embracing universal outlook in contrast to a parochial or narrow outlook. Oddly, the label "Catholic parish" encompasses or embodies both competing energies, and yet the same energy is found in Protestant, Evangelical, Orthodox, Pentecostal, and charismatic expressions of the church. Properly defined and utilized, the role of the Gospel is to ween folks off a tribal and exclusive parochial worldview and introduce to them a more cosmopolitan and inclusive catholic worldview. As James Joyce implies in his book, *Finnegans Wake*, the Catholic Church means 'here comes everybody!'[1]

---

1. Joyce, *Finnegans Wake*. The quote is actually attributed to the Irish-Australian Archbishop Daniel Mannix during World War I. "Finnegans Wake," Wikipedia, http://en.wikipedia.org.

Ecumenical

Like the notion of being "catholic" with a little "c," Christianity Lite is also identified as being more ecumenical than evangelical. Rather than adopting evangelicalism's "one way-ism," ecumenism adopts the "way of one-ism." Ecumenism refers to the twentieth century beginning of a movement toward "unity in diversity" among mainline Protestants. Even today, it consists of autonomous Christians who recognize their vast differences and yet seek to find unity through covenants with one another. Ecumenism suggests that we may not be a united church—and may never be—but we are a *uniting* church still in the process.

If we can acknowledge any connection at all between John's Gospel and the historical Jesus, then we can assume that what mattered most to Jesus in the moments leading up to his betrayal, arrest, trial, torture, and execution was that his followers "be one," a phrase that the writer uses three times in John 17. Jesus wants his followers to be united, which requires faith flexibility rather than faith flexing of muscles. Ecumenical unity, of course, does not always describe Jesus' followers. "Disunited" might be a more appropriate word to use. We need to be frank about the "state of the union" in American Christianity. There is little to no hope of re-uniting the entire Christian church. That ship has sailed, yet even if we don't always have the option of remodeling the ship, we can at least swab the deck.

ONE-ISH

The church should be covenantal, autonomous, catholic, and ecumenical. If we squeeze these four concepts together, we can return to the theme of John 17 and declare that Christians are called to be "one." To be more accurate, they are called to be "one-ish." Being "one" in the sense of being totally united is overrated, because it's just not possible. Followers of Jesus have never been "one in the Spirit" and "one in the Lord" as the popular hymn suggests, although we should aspire to be.[2]

In the New Testament letter to the Ephesians, the writer is obviously aware of disunity, dissension, division, disharmony, and discord within the early church. (There was a lot of "dissing" going on back then—as there is today.) Even then, just a few decades removed from walking and talking with the flesh and blood Jesus, they were not all "one," so the writer

---

2. Peter Scholtes, writer, "They'll Know We are Christians."

Church Polity

encourages the Ephesians (4:3) to make "every effort to maintain the unity of the Spirit in the bond of peace."[3]

Peace and unity are like matching socks. You can't have one without the other. Peace is the glue that keeps us united, and unity, in turn, creates peace. They depend on one another. Unfortunately, any reading of Christian history will tell you that the glue of peace is often in short supply, yet the writer of Ephesians is not about to give up. He is trying to build a unified faith with diverse people, namely Jews *and* gentiles—not an easy assignment. We get that. It's like trying to build a nation of *United* States with people from all over the world. We fail all the time, but we keep trying.

Our quest for oneness didn't begin with the American experiment. The writer of Ephesians is obsessed with oneness. He refers to "one body," "one Spirit," "one hope," "one Lord," "one faith," "one baptism," and, of course, "one God."[4] One, one, one. (Maybe he was numerically challenged and could only count to one!) The writer has high hopes that they can all be on the same page, religiously speaking. He is focused on what "should be" more than what "is," and he wants to be part of an attempt to "knit" together a unified body of Christ "by every ligament," he says.

"Ligament" is a great word to use here because one theory about the origin of the word "religion" is that it comes from the Latin words *re* (again) and *ligament* (the connecting tissue between muscle and bone).[5] Therefore, the word "religion" essentially means to reconnect something that has been broken, severed, or torn apart, like the ligaments in a sprained ankle. Our relationships with God and with one another have been sprained and strained, so we become religious to reconnect. Ephesians addresses the fact that there has already been some tearing apart of the ligaments in the body of Christ. False teachers, to give one example, are tearing apart this infant Christian religion, so the letter tries to connect people, Jews and gentiles, to the same body. It was a worthy goal, although largely unsuccessful.

What about today? Does unity and oneness remain a goal of the Christian faith? Can we be one in the Spirit and one in the Lord after over 2,000 years of being "sprained in the Spirit"? Christianity is so torn apart that we can't even walk the path of Christ together without spraining our ankles, so to speak. Have we been torn apart, sprained, and strained for so long that there is no longer any hope for healing in the body of Christ?

3. Eph. 4:3.
4. Eph. 4:4–6.
5. Wren, "Religion."

We might never be "one in the Spirit" and "one in the Lord," but that's okay because sometimes oneness can be a little cultish. And yet, while being one might be off our radar screens, being "one-ish" seems about right. Being one-ish is not cultish. Perhaps Jesus should have prayed that "they may all be one-ish."

POST-DENOMINATIONAL

Christianity Lite should also maintain a "post-denominational" flavor, not that denominations should become extinct, however. Denominational structures continue to be important and necessary in terms of cultivating new church starts and preparing folks for credentials in ministry, oversight of the process, accountability for both clergy and congregations, providing resources, pooling resources for missions and wider church activities, troubleshooting, support, and encouraging relationships among church leaders and congregations. Unfortunately, the denominational affiliation that is spelled out on the signs in front of local churches might not be all that important to the people in the pews. The history of denominations, including the theological giants and leaders that steered them in a particular direction, is becoming less and less known among the pew-sitters. Nevertheless, behind the scenes denominations continue to provide crucial structural support for the long-term viability of the church.

There are two general "flavors" of denominationalism, one I describe as Heavy and the other as Lite. Heavy-handed Christianity is characterized by top-down hierarchical denominational structures. These denominations produce a heavy presence, one that often squelches the Spirit-inspired freedom of congregations that are serious about pursuing vitality. A post-denominational presence, on the other hand, leaves behind a lighter denominational footprint, one that is not firmly planted on the life force of congregations seeking greater vitality. One's denominational identification is not as important as the way the denominational leaders operate and provide more support than suppression.

I like to think of our connection to denominations using the analogy of riding a bicycle. Catholicism is akin to riding a tricycle—the priests and the papacy provide more laws than liberty. It is difficult for a Catholic congregation or parishioner to feel the wind of the Spirit at their backs. Mainline Protestantism is, to varying degrees, also characterized by a traditionally heavy denominational presence. I compare it to riding a bike with training wheels. Sometimes the congregations and parishioners ride the bicycle on their own, but if they are about to lose control, they have access to denominational parents. Evangelicals are like folks who have largely removed the training wheels and are trying to do it on their own. This is why many of them end up nondenominational.

Speaking of non-denominationalism, I relate them to riding a bike down a hill, letting loose of the handlebars and yelling, "Look ma, no hands!" . . . as they crash into a tree. At first glance, the nondenominational folks seem to reflect what I am calling Christianity Lite to a greater extent than all the rest. However, because they tend to tie themselves less to denominations and more to conservative dogma and charismatic leadership, they suffer from a lack of "brakes," which makes them more vulnerable to a heavy-handed oppressive expression of Christianity.

My response to this analogy is that rather than riding a bike, we should be walking—walking with one another and walking with Jesus—regardless of the sign in front of the church. My definition of post-denominationalism is that it creates a covenantal, autonomous, catholic, and ecumenically-based polity and governance that allows us—individuals and congregations alike—to walk at our own pace, in our own way, and in our own direction, with the Spirit's guidance, of course.

OLD MACDONALD HAD A CHURCH

People often ask me why I chose to move from the Southern Baptist denomination of my youth to the United Church of Christ. Here's what I tell them: *"Old MacDonald had a church, E-I-E-I-O."* After I get a strange look, I then tell them these letters correspond to the five things that attracted me to the United Church of Christ.

The first "E" in Old MacDonald's church stands for *ecumenical*.

The UCC is the most ecumenically minded denomination in the country. It has done as much or more than any other denomination to promote unity among American Christian churches as well as foster relationships with non-Christian religious groups. "That they may all be one," as John's Jesus says.[6] This is our original motto. I was first introduced to the fancy word

---

6. Jn. 17:21.

"ecumenism" in an undergraduate church history class at Hardin-Simmons University in Abilene, Texas, a Baptist school. I still remember the textbook's claim that the United Church of Christ is the flagship denomination of the ecumenical movement. This was the first time I became aware of the UCC. My curiosity was piqued because Southern Baptists are rarely ecumenically minded. Baptists are generally not that interested in Christian unity. This was something new and different for me.

The first "I" in Old MacDonald's church stands for *intelligence*.

In 1987 I graduated with a degree in biblical studies from Hardin-Simmons and then was encouraged to enroll in their master's program in Religion. My encouragement took the form of a full academic scholarship. As the son of two parents that didn't even graduate from high school, I couldn't pass up that opportunity. I decided to major in Old Testament studies. Early in my program, one of my professors took several of his students, including me, to hear the preeminent Old Testament scholar, Walter Brueggemann. Almost everything Dr. Brueggemann said in his lecture series was over my head at the time, yet I was still very much attracted to his creativity, humor, and intelligence. I asked my professor about Dr. Brueggemann's church affiliation. He told me, "The United Church of Christ." *Hmmm, there's that church again.* Later, I discovered that the UCC has a strong history of educated clergy and the founding of respected academic institutions. Intelligence is valued in the UCC.

The second "E" in Old MacDonald's church stands for *ethical*.

Toward the end of my master's program at Hardin-Simmons, I took a course on Christian ethics. After I graduated in 1989, I left Hardin-Simmons to enter a PhD program at another Baptist institution of higher learning, Baylor University. At Baylor I decide to change majors and study Christian ethics. By then I was determined to change my denominational affiliation as well, so I picked up an old-timey phone book and called a local UCC pastor in Robinson, Texas, Ron Krueger. Ron took me to see the South-Central Conference Minister at the time, Jim Tomacek, who took me under his wings and opened the door for me to pastor two rural UCC congregations near Waco, Texas. Being the only UCC pastor in the Baylor Ethics program at that time, many assignments on Reinhold or H. Richard Niebuhr were given to me. These brothers were two of the most preeminent Christian ethicists of the twentieth century and they just happened to have been a part of my new denominational family.

Changing denominations came with its own issues. I phoned my mom shortly after I was called to these two yoked UCC congregations and said to her, "Hey mom, I got a church job." She said, "You got a Baptist church?" I said, "No, mom, I got a UCC church." "What is a UCC church?" she asked. I said, "United Church of Christ." Angrily, she responded, "You're a Church of Christ pastor?" (Southern Baptists and the Church of Christ do not exactly see eye to eye on some things.) I said "No, mom, it's *United* Church of Christ." After a long pause, she asked, "Is that a cult?" No, it's not a cult, yet it is a tradition that takes Christian ethics seriously. As I wrote one research paper after another in the field of Christian ethics, I noticed that UCC scholars are well-represented in the academy.

The second "I" in Old MacDonald's church stands for *independent*.

In the United Church of Christ, although we are called to be in covenant with one another and with all levels of the denomination, we are given an extraordinary amount of freedom. We are decidedly *not* a cult. There is no hierarchy pushing its thumb on us and telling us how to believe nor how to behave. We have a name for this type of church governance: "local church autonomy." Southern Baptists also practice local church autonomy (in theory), so this made my transition to the UCC easier. We do have a denominational structure, yet it is mainly designed to help congregations in such matters as Search and Call for pastors, facilitating fellowship and a sense of unity among its members, providing resources for everything from liturgy to money, and doing cooperative mission work. Also, because we are independent, because we all have what the Baptists call "soul competency," the national face of the UCC, fueled by the General Synod that meets every other year, speaks "to" the church rather than "for" the church on issues that people either agree or disagree with. Anyone with any flexibility at all can live with this kind of independence or autonomy, living in a covenantal context.

Christianity Lite

The "O" in Old MacDonald's church stands for two things:
openness and *oldness*.

At the very least, the openness, of course, refers to the communion table. In the UCC, everyone is invited to the table, not the case in other denominations. This is such an important issue that I tend to break down Christianity into two basic groups: Churches that practice open communion and churches that practice closed communion. I do not consider the latter to be a faithful expression of Jesus' understanding and practice of the Realm of God. I admit I can be a little judgmental about this.

The "O" in Old MacDonald's church also stands for, well, old. Because of its connection to the Congregational churches, which are very numerous in the original American colonies, the UCC is one of the oldest expressions of the Christian faith in the United States. There is a reason why some of our churches are called "Mayflower UCC." This is how I finished that phone conversation with my mom all those years ago. After she asked if this is a cult, I said, "No, mom, it is the oldest church in America." Of course, she responded with, "Well, then, if it's so old how come I've never heard of it?" And I said to her, "Go ask *Old* MacDonald."

8

The Gospel

THE BUNDLE

Years ago, while paying my cable bill, I reflected on the "bundle," a packaged deal that provides our phone, cable, and internet services from the same company. As I was writing the check (in the days before I learned how to pay bills online), I began to see a connection between the Gospel and the Bundle. Each of the three elements of the Bundle—phone, cable, and internet—relate to the Gospel from the perspective of Christianity Lite.

The Landline Phone

The landline is becoming a thing of the past. Most of us have cell or smart phones, therefore the landline phone is becoming obsolete. Still, some people continue to have a landline phone because it offers some important advantages. If we live in the same place for a long time, our landline is the number many people might use to communicate with us. If something happens to our cellphone, such as an accident flushing down the toilet, we still have the landline as a backup. A landline is also useful if we call 9-1-1 because the operator will automatically have our address. Furthermore, if we enjoy being included in surveys or polls, then a landline comes in handy for that as well. This might be one reason polls have been skewed, misleading, or erroneous. Although the landline might be out of date or old-fashioned for some people, for other people it still has a purpose.

The same can be said about the traditional meaning of the Gospel, such as Paul's articulation of it in 1 Corinthians 15:3b-4, "that Christ died for our sins in accordance with the scriptures and that he was buried and that he was raised on the third day in accordance with the scriptures." Traditionally speaking, this is the essence of the Gospel or good news of Jesus Christ: he died for our sins, was buried, and then rose from the dead. Believe in that, and you are good to go. And by "go," I mean die.

Many theologians, preachers, and laypeople today take issue with this definition of the Gospel, especially the notion that Jesus "died for our sins," that he was a blood sacrifice. This makes God look like a blood-thirsty deity; it is one of the most hotly debated theological topics in the church today. As much as we might criticize it, however, it will likely never go away, even if landline phones do. The notion of physical resurrection is also a problem for some because it runs against the clear evidence of science. People that are dead (for more than a few seconds) do not come back to life. For some folks the traditional understanding of the Gospel (atonement and resurrection) is like a landline phone. It had its usefulness in the past, but now that we have gotten smarter (with or without our smart phones), the purpose of the traditional Gospel (like the landline) is being reassessed even as we speak (probably on our cellphones).

Cable Television

Cable television brings us hundreds of channels; most of it is garbage. "Channel surfing" is a thing because people spend much of their time searching for something to watch. It's like a surfer waiting for a good wave to arrive on a calm day. This relates to the Gospel in that there are as many options out there as cable channels. The Gospel is defined, expressed, and practiced in a myriad of ways. Because of that, the Church in the last few centuries has gone the way of Cable television in the last few decades. It has exploded and expanded in a variety of congregational or denominational "channels". Most of it is not worth watching, so church shopping is not much different from channel surfing. It's all about the consumer finding the right product or the right expression of the Gospel for them. If we don't like the way the Gospel is shared, interpreted, or utilized on one channel, that is, in one congregation or denomination (or by televangelists), then we can always turn the channel and find another one.

The Gospel

The Internet

Nothing has revolutionized our world as much as the internet. Most people today can't even remember or imagine what life was like before the internet. And what does the internet do? It gives the average person access to unlimited information. The line between expert and amateur is blurring. The internet is the great equalizer. It has led to the democratization of knowledge. All the world's information is at the tip of our fingers, even if much of it is misinformation.

This modern phenomenon of equal access to information relates to the Gospel as well. What the Gutenberg Press did for access to information in the fifteenth century, including putting the Bible into the hands of laypeople, the internet has done (exponentially more) for access to information today, including information about the Gospel or good news of Jesus Christ.

Not long ago, I downsized my personal theological library, primarily because I no longer need it to find the information I'm looking for. Now, I just google what I'm looking for. This means that you and I have the same degree of access to religious information. The internet has created a democratization of faith. I might wear a robe with three doctor's stripes, but my smartphone isn't smarter than yours. The internet doesn't offer to clergy a higher level of religious knowledge or information. We all have access. One might refer to the internet as an instrument of grace because it levels the playing field for all of us.

So, the next time you think about the Gospel, think of the Bundle and the discount we supposedly receive when we get our phone, cable, and internet from the same company. It might not "save" you in existential terms, but it will save you a bundle . . .

GERM THEOLOGY

The idea for this essay germinated in my reading of John 12:24. Here John's Jesus creatively says, "Very truly, I tell you, unless a grain of wheat falls into the earth and dies, it remains just a single grain, but if it dies, it bears much fruit." The word "grain" in this translation could also be a kernel, seed, sprout, or yes, a germ. A "germ" is a synonym for those other tiny things from which plants arise. I'm not an expert in the agricultural sciences, so I'm not exactly sure how those words are similar or dissimilar. I just know that they all represent the beginning of a plant that, with a little sunshine, water, and encouragement, will soon blossom into life.

Pardon my pun, but what Jesus reportedly says here in John 12:24 is the *kernel* of Christian theology, and that's no small thing. It is the gospel in a nutshell. Jesus uses the common image of a tiny grain of wheat to illustrate how his death will bring life to others. Just as a mature plant dies and scatters its seeds, the Christian faith germinated in Jesus' death and burial (or planting—although he wasn't literally put into the ground—he was put in a pod). In agricultural terms, Jesus's resurrection refers to the blossoming or flowering of what he calls the Kingdom of God. If he had used an agricultural metaphor for "Kingdom of God," he might have called it the "Sod of God." That would play into other agricultural images scattered like seed throughout scripture, such as "sowing and reaping," "the fruit of the Spirit," the "shoot from the stump of Jesse," "the true vine," and "the tree of life," just to name a few.

Based on these words attributed to Jesus in John's gospel, I would like to introduce a new theological term. Taking my cue from science's germ *theory*, I want to introduce a concept called germ *theology*.[1] The premise of germ theology is that Jesus' death, burial (or planting), and resurrection (or flowering) was the beginning of the Kingdom (or Crop) of God taking root in human soil, what we might poetically call the human soul. Since then, it has spread like bluebonnets on Texas roadsides. Germ theology claims God planted a seed in Jesus, and from that seed millions of people have become part of the Sod of God.

According to germ theory, diseases spread when people are *too close* to one another. According to germ theology, the gospel spreads when people are *close enough* to one another. If critics of a heavy-handed expression of Christianity see the Gospel as a contagious disease, I would suggest they find a church that doesn't create "dis-ease" among their people.

EXTENDED WARRANTY

Not long ago, the standard warranty on my pickup was about to expire after six years and one-hundred thousand miles. Suddenly, I began to get a flood

---

1. Germ theory asserts that specific microscopic organisms are the cause of specific diseases. It was developed, proved, and popularized in Europe and North America between 1850 and 1920. Unfortunately, RFK, Jr. doesn't believe germ theory is scientifically valid. Klawans, "A Disproven Medical Theory."

The Gospel

of mail asking me to sign up for an *extended* warranty. To be honest, I don't know if that's a good deal or not. I suppose if it turns out we need it, it's a good deal; if we don't need it, we're just throwing money away. It seems like a toss-up, although there is no doubt that the company that provides the extended warranty is in the business of making money, so they are betting that we will pay more for premiums than they will pay for repairs.

An extended warranty has terms and conditions that might not match the original terms and conditions of the standard warranty. For example, it might not cover anything other than mechanical failure from normal usage, whatever that means. Other exclusions include commercial use of a vehicle, owner abuse, malicious destruction, and ironically "acts of God," which I assume refers to squirrels that are chewing on wires. Anyway, I'm not wise enough to know exactly what to do about this. No doubt my pickup will eventually need some repairs, yet would an extended warranty cover what I need? Should I just risk it and rely on an honest mechanic?

One way to understand Christianity is that it offers an extended warranty for our souls. When we are born, we are given a standard warranty on our bodies, our original "make and model." We are like a new car, straight out of the factory (the womb) and then the car lot (the maternity ward). Everything is shiny and smells good. As the years go by, however, we experience wear and tear on our bodies and minds. As we get older, we need more maintenance. Our bodies are designed to be functional for only a limited amount of time. Eventually, sadly, they will stop working altogether.[2]

The warranty on our physical lives will someday expire, so at some point folks start thinking about an *extended* warranty. This is where religion enters the picture for many people. Quite frankly, the promise of an extended warranty for our lives is why the average age of people in the pews is much higher than the general population. Young people feel invincible. They feel like the standard warranty given at birth is good enough—for now. They are not as concerned as older people about maintenance, other than some largely superficial stuff like using makeup, getting haircuts, or taking a shower here and there. The "muscle cars" among us will work out to improve their overall performance, but for the most part young people are not yet concerned about the general wear and tear on their bodies, much less the end of their functional bodies.

---

2. If our mother's wombs are the factories for our bodies and maternity wards are the car lots for our bodies, then cemeteries are the wrecking yards for our bodies.

On the other hand, the older we get the more obvious it becomes that our original make and model will not last forever, so we begin to turn our attention to the extended warranty our faith promises to provide, the promise that our *spiritual lives*, what some people call our "souls," might possibly last forever. Our scriptures are very specific about this. According to the New Testament, Jesus is the one who makes our extended warranty possible, although the Gospel writers did not think of it in those terms. They didn't have mechanical or electronic items that needed warranties in that place and at that time.[3]

Life informs us that nothing lasts forever, but then Jesus (actually, the church) comes along and offers us an extended warranty, eternal life. All we need to do is *maintain* our spiritual well-being. For instance, communion is like getting an oil change for our souls. Christians understand the bread and wine in the Eucharist in different ways. According to Catholicism, we *literally* consume Jesus' body and blood by ingesting the bread and cup at the Lord's Supper. According to many Protestants, on the other hand, we *symbolically* consume his body and blood at the Lord's Supper. And there are views that lie in between the literal and symbolic. However we interpret it, the gospel writers link this ritual to eternal life, which is like having an extended warranty—an *extremely extensive* extended warranty.

Before Jesus there was already a sense among God's people that God provides some kind of warranty. The Old Testament refers to this as a covenant, an agreement between two parties, in this case God and humanity. The Old Testament covenants, featuring such characters as Noah, Moses, and David, were agreements that if the people are faithful to God, God will be faithful to them. In other words, if they pay the premiums for a warranty, which includes animal and crop sacrifices, God will do the maintenance work—at least for now. It isn't until Jesus comes along, however, that the covenant between God and humanity clearly *extends* beyond our physical lives and is offered to more customers (i.e. gentiles). Jesus ratchets up the notion of covenant.[4] He becomes the "New Covenant." In the gospel of Luke's portrayal of the Lord's Supper in 22:20, for example, Jesus concludes

---

3. However, it wouldn't surprise me if they sometimes guaranteed in writing the performance of their typical mode of transportation, the camel. I'm sure a camel salesman or two must have said to a potential customer, "I can offer a three-year guarantee on this camel over here. It's got good legs and comfortable humps. But it only comes in one color—tan."

4. I hope you enjoyed that pun.

his sharing of bread and wine at the Last Supper with these words, "This cup that is poured out for you is the *new covenant* in my blood."[5]

I suspect many folks join the faith primarily because of the New Covenant or extended warranty that offers hope for eternal life. That's an understandable reason, but it shouldn't be the only reason. It's not like we park our spirituality in the garage waiting until our tags expire to take it out for a spin. There are still roads to travel in *this* life. Eternal life is about *quality* of life (both now and into eternity) as well as *quantity* (or duration) of life. Unfortunately, heavy-handed Christianity often ignores or downplays the qualitative aspect of life and focuses almost exclusively on the quantity. And yet eternal life, as Jesus and the early Christians understood it, begins in the here and now, not the "there and then." Eternal life isn't just about duration; it's about experiencing God's life and purpose in the present moment. We are, at this moment, driving into eternal life in *this* make and model. Christianity Lite doesn't require us to scrap the old car before we go for a ride; it just encourages us to keep up with our maintenance plan.

GOSPEL ON THE GRIDIRON

Have you ever felt as if life is just "piling on"? Your teacher gives you more homework than you can handle. Your boss adds to your workload to the point you feel like quitting. You live in Florida where one hurricane after another comes your way. You get a life-threatening diagnosis. Life has a way of piling on.

When I think of a "pile on" I think of what happens on a football field. Players pile on, not for fun, but for fumbles. The ball pops loose and all hell breaks loose. In a mad scramble for the ball, players pile on top of each other until they are peeled back by the referees. It's a frightening moment for the players at the bottom of the pile, especially if they are claustrophobic. Professional football players talk about feeling stuck. They claim this must be what it feels like to be trapped in rubble after an earthquake, or even to be buried alive. They say there's a lot of fighting, yelling, screaming, eye-gouging, punching, etc. Imagine 330-pound men jumping on top of you.[6]

---

5. Notice that Jesus is borrowing language from Jeremiah 31:31— "The days are surely coming, says the LORD, when I will make a *new covenant* with the house of Israel and the house of Judah."

6. "Nothing Off Limits," NFL.com.

Jesus was not a football player, but he knew how to pile on . . . theologically. We see this in a story from Mark 10. One day a man who seems to have everything going for him encounters Jesus on the road, kneels before him, and asks, "Good Teacher, what must I do to inherit eternal life?" In football terms, this man is trying to find a clear path to the *end zone* without being tackled or fumbling the ball. As a man of means, he probably thinks he already has a clear shot to the end zone since he believes God has blessed him. God has blessed him because he has kept the rules, at least the ones in his playbook, the Torah. He figures he has successfully kept all the rules (or commandments) because he has the evidence. He is a prosperous man with "many possessions." The theological view of that day was if one follows the rules, God will bless that person, and they will prosper. It's just a matter of continuing to follow the rules, that is, running the plays the way the coach, i.e. God, designed them, and they will find the end zone, that is, eternal life.

But questions and doubts have arisen in this man's mind. Although he keeps all the rules—he hasn't committed murder, adultery, theft, lying, or fraud, and he has honored his parents—he still doesn't feel like he is *winning*. He has heard that this teacher, a rabbi from Nazareth, has some new insight, so he asks: "Good Teacher, what must I (a prosperous and blessed man) do to inherit eternal life?" The wording of his question tells me that the man has never had to work a day in his life. He comes from "old money." He sees eternal life as something else to inherit. Other translations use the word "obtain," "get," or "have," rather than "inherit," words that a businessperson might use in this context.

Either way, Jesus is not impressed with this man's self-centered question. Why isn't he asking the same question for all the poor "un-blessed" people who are standing around listening to the conversation. Perhaps for this reason, Jesus decides to tackle him before he gets too close to the end zone. Jesus forces a fumble. He wants the man to let loose of his traditional theological views. And we know what happens when there is a fumble: a pile on!

But not at first. At first, Jesus tries to shoo away the self-righteous man. He tries to run him out of bounds and off the field. There are people here with real problems like starvation and sickness, so he answers the man's question in a dismissive manner: "Just keep following the rules. You'll be fine." As Jesus is turning his attention back to the crowd, the man interrupts. "But Teacher, I've kept all of these (rules) since my youth," implying he still doesn't feel like he's doing it right. At this point, Jesus senses an opening into the man's heart, like a ferocious linebacker eyeing a clear path to an exposed quarterback. The tackle is made, and the ball is loose. Time to pile on. "Okay, then," Jesus says, "You lack one thing; go, sell what you own, and give the money to the poor, and you will have treasure in heaven" (rather than just your bank account). Then you will feel like a winner. Of course, the man is "shocked" because he has "many possessions." Wouldn't we feel the same way?

Do we think Jesus is literally asking the man to sell everything he owns and give to the poor? Yes, but no. Reading between the lines, Jesus is trying to say that none of us, not even the "blessed" among us can get to the end zone by ourselves. We need someone to clear a path for us, to block for us. None of us are "good enough." Jesus even said to the man, "No one is good but God alone."

Jesus continues to pile on theologically by using the analogy of a camel getting through the eye of a needle to illustrate how difficult it is for a wealthy person, a person who is assumed blessed, to thread the needle and get to the end zone. Just as the man was dismayed at Jesus' words, the disciples are perplexed at his words as well.[7] They also erroneously believe that if a person follows all the rules, God will bless them, and they will prosper. This is their goal too. So, with sincere confusion they ask, "Then who can be saved?" If those who are blessed and prosperous are not good enough, then none of us have the chance of a snowball in hell. You're right, Jesus says. It is impossible for you to make it to the end zone by your own merit, and yet God makes it possible.

What's Jesus doing here? Playing mind games? No, I think it's very simple. If we try to run with the ball by ourselves, we will not make it to the end zone. We need God. Simple as that. It is about as basic a message as Jesus has ever delivered, and yet it is a message that upends everything.

Peter has been listening to this entire conversation. He watches the rich man fumble the ball, so he tries to recover it for his team: "Look, Jesus, me and my fellow disciples have already done what you are asking this rich guy to do. We have left everything and followed you. We can already thread that needle." Jesus admires Peter's attempt at a fumble recovery. He affirms that anyone who sacrifices everything for Jesus' sake will receive back a hundredfold what they have sacrificed. But here's where Jesus continues

---

7. There is the view that the "eye of a needle" is a reference to a small door in Jerusalem called "the Needle's Eye." For a camel to go through this door, all the bulky possessions tied to the camel would have to be removed first. Hence, it is difficult for a person with wealth and possession to take them through the eye of a needle.

to pile on: Peter, on your way to the end zone (eternal life) you will also be persecuted. It will feel like you are at the bottom of a pile of 330-pound men. And just so Peter doesn't think he is really any better than the rich man, Jesus piles on once again with the Mother of All Pile-Ons. He says, "But many who are first will be last, and the last will be first." If Peter had any air in his lungs from the pile on, this would be the final blow.

Jesus is saying that when we think we are heading for the end zone, that we've got a clear path to eternal life, chances are we're heading for the wrong end zone. This reminds me of a game between the San Francisco 49ers and the Minnesota Vikings on October 25, 1964. The Vikings' defensive end, Jim Marshall, picks up a 49ers fumble and runs all the way to the wrong end zone, resulting in a two-point safety for the 49ers. It was one of the worst plays in NFL history. It is also the story of humanity, lost and aimless.

So, what is this story all about in Mark 10? It is about our common faulty theological assumptions about the gospel. If we think we are good enough to "inherit" eternal life because we have followed all the rules and kept all the commandments, prayed the proper prayers, been baptized in the right mode at the right age, received the bread and cup from the Lord's Table, read the Bible from cover to cover, joined a "Bible believing" church, given our tithes and offerings, volunteered, witnessed to other folks about our faith, or whatever it might be . . . if we think any of that is good enough, we are probably heading for the wrong end zone. I'm not talking about "eternal hell," just that our lack of humility is showing. Despite the evangelically oriented theme of this story, the underlying message is very much in the vein of Christianity Lite: a stance of humility and uncertainty is preferable to a stance of haughtiness and certainty.

9

Spirituality

COP-OUT, COVER-UP, OR CATCH-ALL

I HAVE COME UP with a brief little questionnaire to test our faith. There are three questions we can ask ourselves, which are:

1. Is my faith a cop-out?
2. Is my faith a cover-up?
3. Is my faith a catch-all?

First, is my faith a cop-out? A "cop-out" is an avoidance of commitment or responsibility. It is an evasion, an escape from facing up to something. Sadly, this is the role that faith occasionally plays for the anti-intellectual and insincere. Faith becomes an excuse for ignorance: "I don't have to know about or understand (fill in the blank) because I have faith. Faith is all I need." That may be true, but it still sounds like a cop-out. Faith needs to be a little smarter than that.

Second, is my faith a cover-up? A "cover-up" means to hide the truth about something unethical or illegal. Historically, heavy-handed Christians have used their faith to cover up a multitude of things that are unethical, even sinful, such as racism ("slavery is supported by scripture") or sexism ("women should remain silent in church"), not to mention pedophilia. Our faith has been used repeatedly to cover-up many other "isms" out there. We need to stop that. Faith needs to be better than that.

Finally, is my faith a catch-all? A "catch-all" is something that is designed to address a variety of situations or possibilities. In this view, faith should permeate, pervade, and penetrate everything we do or say. It should be our T.O.E.—our "theory of everything"—albeit with a lite footprint. As a catch-all, it should be our hook, line, and sinker. I prefer this all-encompassing way of understanding and practicing our faith. It maintains the *mystery* of faith even as it implies the *mastery* of faith. It is through faith that we navigate every aspect of our spiritual journeys.

At times, however, the only thing we seem to be catching is doubt. We are saddened if not haunted by our doubts about the things of God, so we tell ourselves that we need to toss our doubts over the side of the boat and keep fishing for faith. We see faith and doubt in opposition to one another, as part of a zero-sum game; if faith is winning, then doubt is losing, or vice versa. We rarely consider the notion that they can exist side-by-side as partners in our spirituality.

"Doubting Thomas" is often resurrected in our discussions when considering this false dichotomy of faith and doubt. This is an unfortunate label for Thomas, but it is understandable. Thomas is unwilling to believe his friends when they tell him that Jesus appeared to them after he died on a cross. Why *would* anyone believe that? If any of the other disciples had been absent when Jesus appeared earlier, they also would have had their doubts. Let's not forget that they were in one place out of fear that the same people who crucified Jesus would come after them. Thomas, on the other hand, had the courage to be out and about. We tend to think Jesus chastises Thomas later for believing (i.e. faith as mental assent) only after he has physical proof, but the other disciples believe only after they have proof as well. So, we should be easy on Thomas. Elsewhere in the gospel accounts, such as John 11:5–16, he is a person of passionate faith.

In Christianity Lite, faith and doubt are two sides of the same coin. They keep one another honest. For faith to be a "catch-all," doubt needs to be part of the bait. Faith needs doubt so that one doesn't become too gullible, and doubt needs faith so that one doesn't become too hopeless. We need faith that is both honest and open, and we need doubt that is grounded in integrity and curiosity.

ON TRACK

My favorite comedians are those who employ "observational humor." People like Jerry Seinfeld and Jim Gaffigan are great at it. I aspire to be the preacher equivalent of an observational comedian. By that, I mean that I enjoy observing simple, everyday events in life and using these observations

Spirituality

to mine spiritual lessons and share them in my preaching and writing. I am constantly observing ordinary events that can teach us something about faith and spirituality. When I'm sitting in my backyard in Central Texas, for example, I think about such things as the wind and sun, the live oak trees, birds and bugs, houses and roads, etc.—all sermon material, and all easily ignored if not on the lookout for such things. The one thing I can't ignore while sitting in my backyard, however, is the train tracks that rest across the street from my home. It's difficult to ignore the train.[1]

I have learned some important spiritual lessons from listening to and observing the train and the train tracks. The first thing that occurs to me as I lounge in my backyard is that sometimes I have a *one-track mind*. A one-track mind is a phrase that comes from the fact that a train runs only on one track at a time in one direction. Fortunately, I don't have the same one-track mind I had when I was a teenager. That would get me into a lot of trouble at my current age, but I am the kind of person that can get preoccupied with a particular topic or activity. My one-track mind has fixated on such things as a particular band or musician, a particular author, a sports team or two, important social issues, and yes, theological quandaries. The one track that my adult life has traveled the most is the railroad of religion. At this point, I've ridden too far to even consider hopping off that train. I do get on other tracks from time to time, but the railroad of religion has been the most traveled track of both my personal and professional life. Concerning my professional life, some days I feel as confident as a conductor while at other times I feel as humbled as a hobo. (Are we still allowed to use the word "hobo"?)

The second thing that occurs to me as I watch the train parading past the parsonage is that we religious folks like to talk about being on a spiritual "path" or "journey," which is another way of saying we are on a *spiritual track*. Hopefully we are "on track" or going in the right direction. If I may degrade myself with a moment of binary thinking, there are two kinds of Christians in the world: Those who see spirituality as a continuing journey, with open-ended tracks (a characteristic of Christianity Lite), and those who believe they have already reached the train station. I much prefer to be a pastor to folks who believe they are still "on track" rather than those who

---

1. This is especially true for me because the so-called Railway Killer murdered one of my colleagues and his spouse in our parsonage in May 1999. The train is a constant reminder of that tragic event.

believe they have already reached their destination. I can't help those who believe they have already "arrived." I know I haven't.

The third thing that occurs to me as my ear drums are bursting from the sound of the blaring horn is that sometimes we get *sidetracked* on our spiritual journeys. Another way to say this is we often get *distracted*. We may not get so distracted that we fall off the rails, but human nature being what it is we can easily get sidetracked, meaning our attention to our spiritual journey can lose focus or be diverted from its main purpose. Life has a way of persuading us to switch tracks, without slowing down.

This is true even for religious professionals like me. We can get as sidetracked as anyone. A case in point are the religious professionals in first century Judaism known as the Sadducees, who become distracted about the marital status of a woman who had married seven brothers: "In the resurrection . . . whose wife will the woman be?" they ask Jesus. They are being disingenuous because they don't even believe in the resurrection of the dead. Their intent is to sidetrack or distract Jesus from the Law of Moses, and yet, like other stories in the Gospels, it backfires on them: "Those who are considered worthy of a place in that age and in the resurrection from the dead neither marry nor are given in marriage." This sends the sad Sadducees backtracking.[2]

We do the same sort of thing, do we not? We get sidetracked on our spiritual journeys with irrelevant theological questions or concerns. We go off on tangents. We major in minor issues even as we minor in major issues. We lose focus on what is most important, which is *love* in all its many manifestations. The message of the Bible is God loves us, Jesus loves us, so love God and Jesus, love your neighbors (as much as you love yourselves), and love your enemies. That last one is the one that bugs people. Still, we should not *lose track* of the love bug.

PORTFOLIOS

"You can't take it with you when you die." That's what everyone says, and for the most part, they are right. We aren't like the ancient kings who were buried with their possessions, if not their pets, servants, and wives. We enter this world with nothing, and we leave it with nothing. Sometimes our inability to take everything with us begins before we pass on. I recently witnessed this while helping my mom leave her home and move into a

2. Lk. 20:27–40.

Spirituality

retirement residence, which is much smaller than her home. She had to give away or sell probably ninety-five percent of her possessions. She knew she couldn't take it with her anyway.

The phrase, "You can't take it with you" was made popular in 1936 as the title of a play by George Kaufman and Moss Hart and a 1938 film based on that play.[3] This is interesting because they were written and produced during the Great Depression when people had fewer things to take with them!

"You can't take it with you" has become for some people a warning against materialism. Since we can't take it with us, we shouldn't attach too much importance to money and possessions. For other people, however, it sends the opposite message: Since we can't take our money and possessions with us into the next life, we might as well accumulate and enjoy ourselves as much as possible in this life. Either way, the first thing St. Peter says to us when we arrive at the Pearly Gates is, "Your money is no good here, sir (or ma'am)."

Regardless of one's personal philosophy about money and possessions, if we are honest with ourselves, we would admit that we would love to have "more" or "as much as we want" in the here and now. One of the ways people do this is by investing. The word "invest" has an interesting history. Literally, it means "to clothe." This makes sense because in the old world the best way to show wealth was not the make and model of one's automobiles, country club memberships, or stock portfolios. The best way to show wealth was by the clothes they wore. Even today, we tell people to "dress for success." This is a practical and literal way to invest.

These days, investing consists of many more layers (if you will excuse the clothing pun). To be a successful investor, one needs to know about such things as mutual funds, stocks, bonds, CD's, savings accounts, money market accounts, IRA's, retirement plans, dividends, trusts, etc. If one is feeling particularly frisky and risky, there are cryptocurrencies, which I understand as much as I understand artificial intelligence or rocket science. "Crypto" is a Greek word that means "hidden, secret, or covered," which automatically makes me suspicious about cryptocurrencies. "Crypto" is related to another Greek word, "crypta," or "vault," which is a stone chamber beneath the floor of a church or other building that typically contains coffins and other religious relics. So, yes, cryptocurrency supporters might be

---

3. "You Can't Take It With You," produced and directed by Frank Capra, Columbia Pictures..

trying to say that you *can* take it with you, that your money will be good in the crypt. Not true, although it might get you a nicer crypt.

We can't take our money and possessions with us, we can't impress St. Peter with our stock portfolios, but we can take *something* with us when we die. We can take our *soul* portfolios, what we have invested in our inner selves, our spiritual lives, rather than material things. This will either be true in the sense of an "after life," or in the sense of the footprint, legacy, and memories we leave behind. The point is, we won't leave this world empty-handed. We might not take with us what we have, but we will take with us *who we are*. So, we should invest in who we are as much or more than in what we have.

In one of Jesus' parables found in Mark 4:26–29, he uses the analogy of seeds scattered on the ground. If you think about it, farming is the act of *investing* seeds in the ground. The seeds, like money in the stock market, seem to lie dormant, doing nothing we can see, but then one day they sprout and grow into a full head of grain. This is a parable about investing our faith in God's future, investing or planting our souls in "the Sod of God," what Jesus calls the Kingdom of God. It is a parable about investing in our soul portfolio.

Mark 4:30–32 is the famous mustard seed parable. This is also a parable about spiritual investing. We begin where we are in our spiritual journey, as tiny and insignificant and unworthy as it might seem and invest our inner lives in the Sod of God. The investment of that tiny seed "pays off," symbolized by the "greatest of all shrubs." What we have planted in the heart of God is what we will take with us.

An interesting side note here is that investing our actual monetary resources is conversely an *act of faith*. We must have some level of faith or trust in our stockbroker or the stock market. It's sort of like gambling, but the difference between gambling and investing is that gambling expects either an immediate return or loss. Investing, on the other hand, requires long-term patience and perseverance. It also expects either a return or a loss, but not immediately. If done wisely, the odds of a return on our investments are much better than the odds of a lottery ticket, a poker hand, or a bet on the horses.

We can apply this to the difference between gambling and investing *in a spiritual context*. In the seventeenth-century, there was a French thinker named Blaise Pascal. Pascal argued that whether we are aware of it or not, we are all gambling on whether God exists. We refer to his famous argument as "Pascal's Wager." The way he describes this wager is complicated, but I will simplify it. Pascal said that a rational person will bet their lives on God. A thoughtful person will believe in God and adopt a faithful lifestyle, one that rejects the pursuit of worldly things like money and possessions. He based his argument on the potential outcomes of this spiritual wager. If God does not exist, the faithful person will only suffer the loss of certain pleasures and luxuries in this life. No big deal. Even if God doesn't exist the religious person can still have a meaningful life. However, if God *does* exist, the faithful person will stand to gain on their "investment" in a considerable way; namely (according to Pascal), the blessings of heaven, as opposed to the sufferings of hell if one makes a wager against God's existence. So, whether God exists or not, said Pascal, our best bet is to lay down a few bucks on God's existence. God is a good bet. Pascal's Wager is not exactly how I would go about trying to convince folks to plant a few seeds in the Sod of God. I'm not a fan of scare tactics, but I do believe that our best bet is to invest in our soul portfolios.

We should also consider *diversifying* our soul portfolios. We shouldn't put all our eggs in one basket, as heavy-handed faith mandates. Our soul portfolios should be much more extensive than dogmatic beliefs in God. To diversify, we should spread our seeds liberally, investing in God *and* goodness, faith *and* families, religion *and* relationships, spirituality *and* society, Creator *and* creation. There are all sorts of investments we can make in our soul portfolios, things that will "pay off" someday in this life and/or the next.

LIFE+

When I think about the mystery of life, I have one foot in science and the other in religion (although I admit I have a deeper understanding of religion). I am aware of the conflict between science and religion. Some people see them in opposition to one another, but I don't. I see them as complementary, even when they seem to be at odds with one another. My philosophy has always been "truth is truth no matter where we find it," so I try to go through life open to where the breadcrumbs of truth lead me.

Scientists have more than a few things to say about how life originated. Although they claim the universe began with the "Big Bang" nearly 13.8 billion years ago, living things did not appear on planet Earth until about three billion years ago. That's more than a ten-billion-year gap when

Earth consisted of little more than dead rocks and lifeless oceans. (Not a very inviting place.) How life finally emerged remains a mystery. Did God *speak* it all into existence as the book of Genesis suggests? Was it a strike of lightning that somehow provided the spark needed for life to begin? Did carbon and hydrogen merge together after spewing out of deep-sea vents creating the first living creatures? Was life brought here from somewhere else in the galaxy, perhaps even from Martian meteorites?[4]

What about consciousness? When and how did living creatures first "wake up" or become conscious or sentient? One of the most prominent theories is that consciousness began when animals such as birds and mammals developed larger brains around two hundred million years ago. The first humans didn't emerge until a few hundred thousand years ago, give or take a few minutes. So, is life and consciousness a fluke? A once-in-the-lifetime-of-a-universe phenomenon? Is it found only on this planet, or does it exist elsewhere in the universe?

So many questions . . . and not enough answers. I'm inclined to go with the famous quote attributed to Søren Kierkegaard: "Life is not a problem to be solved, but a reality to be experienced." Part of that experience—a big part for many of us—is *religion*. Our faith also has a few things to say about the mystery of life, although science wasn't even a thing when the Creation stories were written in the book of Genesis about 2,500 years ago. The bible is not a textbook—it's a faith book. The founders of our faith were not yet familiar with many of the questions about life's origins, much less the answers. And so, as one of my Old Testament professors once said: "The Bible doesn't tell us *how* God created the world. It just tells us *that* God created the world." And as God said, "It was good."

When I think of the relationship between science and religion, I look at it this way: Religion takes life's question to another level. Even before science can answer all its questions, religion has the audacity to expand the questionnaire. I can envision science and religion as the two main topics of two separate streaming services on our televisions. In my scenario, science would be the *Life* channel, and religion would be the *Life+* channel.

Have you ever noticed how many Life+ words and phrases are used in our religion? Much like the word "religion" itself, there are many words that begin with the prefix "re," which means "again." One of the popular theories about the origin of the word "religion" is that it came from the

---

4. If so, does that suggest Mars is the original Garden of Eden?

110

Spirituality

Latin word *relegere*, which means "go through again."[5] The implication is that religion is the vehicle that takes us through life again in the sense of a new beginning. We use words like "repentance," which means to review one's life and redirect it—to go in a different direction. Religion is a reassessment, recalibration, and renewal of life. It is like hitting the reset button on our electronic equipment, hoping that life will reboot in a fuller way. Religion is Life+. It is all about being reborn or born again, revived, and restored. Religion gives us a chance to live again. It even has the audacity to claim that life can be eternal— "everlasting life."

Life is awesome in and of itself. There is no Life+ without Life. Even so, Life+ goes beyond Life in several ways. First, at the risk of being repetitive, Life+ tells us that life can be restored, rebirthed, and reenergized. We see this vividly in Ezekiel 37:1–14, the "valley of the dry bones." During the Babylonian Exile, the prophet Ezekiel has a vision of the restoration of the people of Israel. The setting of the vision is that of a battlefield filled with the bones of dead soldiers, clearly an image of defeat and death. In Ezekiel's vision of the future, however, God breathes new life into those old dry bones after Ezekiel graphically describes a rattling noise as the bones come together, along with new sinew and flesh. This is a vision of Israel's rebirth, and it plays a big role in ancient Judaism and Christianity's understanding of a future resurrection of the dead. Life+ tells us that our lives, no matter how dry our spiritual bones are, can be restored, rebirthed, reenergized, revived, and revitalized.

Furthermore, Life+ tells us that life is more than just a material or physical phenomenon. It can be infused with the Spirit. In Paul's writings, he makes a clear distinction between life in the flesh, which is all-too-often bound to sin and death, and life in the spirit (Life+). We should be careful drawing a hard line between flesh and spirit; they are both to be celebrated. Again, there is no Life+ without Life. Life in the flesh is precious, valuable, and worthy of our care. Yet, Paul is claiming that religion is like going to the hospital for an IV of the Spirit. Through our faith we are infused with the Spirit. The Spirit dwells in us and gives new life to our mortal bodies just as the Spirit raised Jesus from the dead.

Life is a mystery. The answers continue to elude us, mainly because we don't even know all the questions. But Kierkegaard was right: "Life is not a problem to be solved, but a reality to be experienced." I think he was referring to both Life and Life+.

---

5. "Religion," Online Etymology Dictionary (noun), http://www.etymonline.com.

10

Prayer

A PIECE OF CAKE

Heavy-handed prayer warrior types understand and practice prayer as if it's a piece of cake, topped with a thick spread of frosty guilt if one doesn't include a large degree of certainty in one's recipe. Christianity Lite understands and practices prayer as if it might turn out to be an upside-down cake—by accident. Due to my tendency to dig down deeply into theological rabbit holes, prayer raises more questions for me than it answers. For example, should we expect answers to our prayers? If there is no answer, is that necessarily a "no" answer, as people often claim? If a prayer seems to have been answered, could it be a mere coincidence or, as the writer Squire Rushnell claims, are we receiving a "God wink"?[1] Theologians might ask why we should pray in the first place. If God is all-knowing, doesn't God already see what's on our minds? And for what should we pray? Health and wellbeing. Job security or promotions? Homeruns or touchdowns? Victory in war? Good parking spots? Where do we draw the line between appropriate and inappropriate prayers? Or does that even matter?

The Apostle Paul was either just pulling our legs or he was less confused about prayer than we are. Either way, in 1 Timothy 2:1–2, he mentions various categories of prayer and suggests we should pray for "everyone," which, oh, I don't know, kind of makes the whole prayer thing potentially burdensome. Interestingly, he emphasizes praying for "all who are in high

1. Rushnell, "When God Winks." A God wink is defined as "an event or personal experience, often identified as coincidence, so astonishing that it is seen as a sign of divine intervention, especially when perceived as the answer to a prayer." "God-wink Definition," YourDictionary, http://www.yourdictionary.com.

positions," because it's worthwhile to create goodwill between those at the top and those at the bottom of the food chain. People usually respond well when they know people are sending "thoughts and prayers" their way.[2]

At the end of the day, and likely from now until the end of all my days, I will continue to struggle with questions about prayer. However, there are times I think to myself that one reason it all seems so hard is because we are looking for answers that replace the question marks, commas, and semi-colons with hard-and-fast periods. This might not be the best thing that can happen to people who are trying to grow, change, and evolve in a productive way.

In the meantime, let's cut one another some slack. We're all just trying to figure out how to think about and do things that are next to impossible. We're all doing the best we can with the tools we have, which means that sometimes, unbeknownst to us, we are using the wrong tools. And on the rare occasion when something feels like a cakewalk, say a prayer for those who can't walk, forget to bring a cake, or would rather have pie.

READER'S DIGEST

You're waiting in the lobby of a doctor's office. You forgot to bring your cell phone with you, so you have nothing to do. There's a cooking show on the little television on the wall, but the sound is turned all the way down. As you scan the room for potential entertainment, your eye spots some out-of-date, seen-their-better-days magazines on a little table nestled between two other people waiting for their names to be called. They are both on their phones, one watching annoying TikTok videos and the other updating their social media posts. Shyly and slyly, you approach the table and spot a *Better Homes and Gardens* (that looks like every other *Better Homes and Gardens*), a *Sport's Illustrated* that features the uninteresting Winter Olympic games from several years ago, a health magazine of some sort with a buff twenty-something-year-old on the cover (so you know it's not for you), and, surprisingly, a copy of *Reader's Digest*. Why hasn't anyone pocketed this little pocketbook? Looking for a way to pass the time, you quickly grab the *Reader's Digest*, walk back to your seat, take the Word Power Vocabulary Quiz, hear your name called, follow the nurse to your room, and,

---

2. Unless a mass shooting has occurred, then nix the "thoughts and prayers" language because that phrase is as empty as the hole a bullet creates in a person's skull.

knowing you will be sitting in *that* room for a while, pull from your pocket the *Reader's Digest* that you just lifted from the lobby.

No idle time for you. Time is money. The most successful people in the world use every spare minute at their disposal to learn something new or do something productive. Human beings have always been this way. Although our ancestors didn't have all the things we enjoyed keeping ourselves occupied, I'm convinced they sought to use their time wisely and productively. We live in a very different world from our ancestors; we have a myriad of choices to keep us active, so I have a theory about this. I believe that the one activity that has suffered the most in recent history because of all the choices we have to keep us occupied is *prayer*. The busier we are the less we pray. The more we play the less we pray. There is no way to prove this, but I am convinced that prayer has taken a back seat to everything else we have invented to occupy our spare time in this modern world. We have sidelined our main line to God. But it wasn't always this way.

Put yourself in the sandals of Jesus' first disciples. What did they do all day? Fish? Sit in the shade? Gaze at the stars? Tell tall tales? As they were busy trying to survive, they were not distracted all day long by shiny objects. I suspect they occupied much of their time *talking to God or their gods*. If an alien had witnessed this, they might have concluded that Homo sapiens spends much of their time talking to the air in a variety of postures: heads bowed, eyes closed, arms raised, knees bent, or in a lotus position (a position my body simply refuses to take). The alien might ask why we pray and what we hope to gain by it, and the answers might vary. Some of us believe in directly answered prayers, if not outright miracles, while others see prayer as akin to punting in a football game. When all else fails, pray, and hope for the best. At the very least, we believe prayer puts us in better "field position" with God.

His disciples noticed that Jesus was one of those prayer warrior types—he prayed like he was about to go to war. It was serious business. So, one day, while they were watching his intensity, they said to him, "Lord, teach *us* to pray, as John taught his disciples." This might have been a subtle criticism of Jesus's lackadaisical approach to teaching about prayer, at least compared to John the Baptist's obvious fervency.

I understand the need for a lesson or two on prayer, especially from an expert like Jesus. When are we supposed to pray? Before we eat? Before we go to bed? Before we go bungee jumping? Where should we pray? In public restaurants? In prayer closets? At the 50-yard line before or after a high school football game? How should we pray? Should we be concerned about theological correctness or the length of our prayers? Should we incorporate a few words from the King or Queen's English (e.g., "thee" and "thou") to impress God? For whom should we pray? Ourselves? Our loved ones? Our enemies? *To* whom should we pray? God? Jesus? The Holy Spirit? Mother Mary? The Saints?

I don't know which of these questions the disciples may have had in mind when they asked Jesus to teach them to pray, but Jesus offers what we Protestants call the Lord's Prayer, and the Catholics refer to as the Our Father. The version we recite in worship every Sunday is a combination of Matthew's and the Didache's version. The Didache was a popular early Christian document, but not part of our Bibles. Luke's version is more of a Reader's Digest version, shorter than the other two. There are also translation issues, such as whether to use the words "debts," "trespasses," or even "sins."[3] I always smile when the Lord's Prayer is recited at a funeral, and everyone is praying their favored version. The cacophony is only outdone when we recite the Lord's Prayer together at a Zoom meeting.

After Jesus recites this prayer to them, the disciples must have thought, "Gee, he must be giving us the short version. When he goes off by himself to pray, he is there for much longer than that!" The Lord's Prayer, I believe, is meant to be a prayer primer and not a primetime prayer. It is not meant to be the entirety of our prayer life, but a spark or an ignition switch. We should imagine this as Jesus' first lesson on prayer in his introductory course to a spiritual life. The first thing we notice about this prayer is its brevity and simplicity of language. He doesn't use fancy and formal language. He uses the language of the people. He uses the word *Abba*, a familiar and informal rendering of "father".[4]

The other thing we notice about the Lord's Prayer is that it is hope-filled. It's not judgmental, accusatory, wrathful, or anything of the sort. Instead, it encourages us to pray for things that are necessary for those who are heavily invested in a spiritual journey: bread or sustenance, forgiveness of sins, the ability to forgive everyone indebted to us, and the avoidance of being tried or tempted. That sounds simple, but this is an aggressive agenda. We could spend an entire lifetime praying and hoping that these few things

---

3. Lk. 11:2–4. Notice that Luke uses "sins" and "indebted".

4. Jesus uses the masculine term, *Abba*, not because God is literally a male. That would be silly. He uses that term, rather than a female term, because it was culturally appropriate in that place and time to do so. We shouldn't get hung up on that issue.

become a reality in our lives. Jesus is telling his disciples (and us) that if we are going to take time out of our busy schedules to pray, we might as well go all in. Why beat around the bush?

In our place and time, with our busy, distracting schedules, the Lord's Prayer should be something we can pull out of our pockets at a moment's notice. Commercial breaks, stop lights, waiting in the drive-thru line, on hold on the telephone, bathroom breaks, taking a shower, waiting for the microwave or oven ding or the toaster pop-up, waiting for the Uber driver to arrive, the school bell to ring in the morning, the nurse to come take you to the next waiting room . . . Wherever you might be enjoying some down time these days, make sure you always have a prayer in your back pocket.

RULING THE RANDOM

I have had the same job title for over three-and-a-half decades, so I think it's about time I get a promotion. Not a raise; just a promotion. I honestly don't know what that would look like, what my new title would be, or how my job description would change. I just feel like I've hit the proverbial glass ceiling in my profession. I'm kidding, of course. I'm in one of those professions where there is very little room for advancement unless one is in a big church with multiple staff, then maybe. There's very little wiggle room in this line of work. If I do a great job, it's not like I can get some kind of upper management job in a corner office on the top floor, and if I do a poor job, it's not like I can be demoted to the mailroom or go back down to the Minor League of Pastors and work on my preaching (not pitching). I'm sort of stuck right where I am, which I enjoy immensely.

Because of my stagnant-oriented career choice, I can't relate very well to what two men in Acts 1 are going through as they vie for a prized promotion, to be selected as the next apostle. There is an opening on this board of apostles because one of the original twelve, Judas Iscariot, has gone rogue. Judas took a bribe from a competing company, betrayed his boss, Jesus of Nazareth, and then felt so guilty about it, he hung himself. The book of Acts adds that he died in a grotesque manner in the piece of property he purchased with the bribe money.[5] That's the kind of irony Alanis Morrisette would appreciate.[6]

---

5. Acts 1:18.

6. Morrisette, "Ironic," from the album *Jagged Little Pill*, Maverick & Warner Bros, 1996.

Prayer

After the death of Judas and their CEO, this young startup company needs to find a way to get back on their feet. Their by-laws state they need a twelve-member board of directors, so they hold a meeting to determine who will fill the expired man's unexpired term. They look over their company roster and spot two men who stand out for their loyalty to the company and for their capability as effective salesmen, that is, witnesses to the Resurrection.

I might be reading into this a little too much, but it seems as if the first man they propose has a bit of a sketchy past. I say that because he has a couple of aliases. He is listed as Joseph called Barsabbas, who is also known as Justus. Well, which is it? "Barsabbas," by the way, like the "Barabbas" who was released when Jesus was arrested, literally means "son of the father." Today, we would call this man "Junior." He is obviously named after his father, whether his father was Joseph or Justus. Nevertheless, this uncertainty about his name is probably a red flag for the board of apostles. The other gentleman the board recommends is Matthias, a man with no known aliases.

Now the board has the task of choosing one of the two nominees. How do they do it? Vetting someone in that era was not easy. It's not like they could Google a name, call their references, or examine their social media posts. So, they choose their twelfth man the old fashion way, by pure chance. Or was it? They cast lots. Like a lottery, casting lots seems so random for something so important. We don't know exactly how they cast lots. It could have been something like drawing straws, picking a card, flipping a coin, spinning a wheel, or maybe even spinning the bottle. Whatever it was, they do not see it as a random act. Before they cast lots to see which of these two men will be selected, they pray: "Lord, you know everyone's heart. Show us which one of these two you have chosen to take the place in this ministry and apostleship from which Judas turned aside to go to his own place."

They believe that the Lord, the Creator of the heavens and the earth, will guide, if not control, the outcome of this random act of casting lots. We might think this is unsophisticated bad theology, but we can't fault them for faulty theology. They don't have two-thousand years of academically oriented theological reflection under their belts. All they have is a sincere and heartfelt trust in the One who has seen them through the most difficult time of their lives—the death of their founder and CEO, Jesus of Nazareth—and then the most surprising moment of their lives—the resurrection and exaltation of Jesus. After witnessing all of that, why *wouldn't* they believe that God rules the random? Thus, when the lot points to Matthias they do not hesitate to add his name to the board of apostles. They might have even given him Judas's old job as treasurer. (So, off to the bank they go to get his name on a signature card.)[7]

Since Matthias is never mentioned again in the New Testament, this story seems sort of insignificant, and yet I think it is a story that provides great insight into the way people *trust* in God. Yes, they may be a little naïve to think that God will control the outcome of a spin of the bottle or a drawing of straws, but in a world of complexity and uncertainty, does it really hurt to rely on and trust in the Creator of the Universe to rule the random moments of our lives?

Some things, of course, just seem too unimportant for God's rule. For example, I must admit that I'm not prone to pray for a perfect parking spot. I'm not likely to leave it to the Lord if I buy a lottery ticket. I'm not inclined to beg God for better bargains in the big box stores or demand the deity to determine the destiny of the Dallas Cowboys. Some things just seem too trivial for God's attention. However, if I know someone is suffering, I will solicit the Savior. If there is violence in the world or in our communities, I will petition for peace. If there is conflict in our culture, I will call on the Creator. To be honest, I don't know where to draw the line between what's important enough to ask God to intervene or interfere and what isn't. But here's what I want to say: *It doesn't matter.*

From a Christianity Lite perspective, it doesn't matter if we draw the line in the wrong place. We have and we will. I would rather err on the side of naively trusting in God than talking myself out of talking to God. If God is too busy or too big to worry about my petty little problems, then so be it. Nothing ventured, nothing gained. If God had nothing to do with Matthias' choice to fill the vacant apostle's seat on the board, I don't think it matters one bit. Hopefully, with or without God's help, Matthias turned out to be a good choice. But, yeah, if I were able to plead with providence for a promotion, I would probably give it a go, as self-centered as that might sound. Our prayer life doesn't suffer because we ask for too much. It suffers because we ask for too little.

7. Acts 1:23–26.

11

Evangelism

OPENS DOORS, MINDS, AND HEARTS

Mottos are windows into the souls of denominations. There are several associated with my denomination, the United Church of Christ, such as "That they may all be one," "God is still speaking," and "No matter who you are or where you are on life's journey, you are welcome here." The newest one is "A just world for all," which inspired one UCC minister to say that maybe our next motto should be: "We collect mottos." If so, I think our next motto should be "Less mottos, more motion." Other examples of denominational mottos, often tongue in cheek, include this one for the Christian Church (Disciples of Christ): "We agree to disagree agreeably." The Presbyterians are known for their "decently and in order" battle cry (admittedly not the most inspiring motto ever produced . . . but you figure your children would be safe around them). Someone on social media suggested a reimagining of the Southern Baptist Convention's acronym: "SBC: Still Belongs to the Confederacy."

One of my favorite mottos belongs to the United Methodists: "Open hearts. Open minds. Open doors." A welcoming posture is the hoped-for result of this epigram.[1] Almost everyone wants to be perceived as a welcoming congregation or denomination. But how do we get there? How does a church or denomination, United Methodist or otherwise, become a church with hearts, minds, and doors that are truly open and not just part of a slogan? I am reminded of the Apostle Paul's words to one of the

---

1. Apparently, not all Methodists have the same attitude, evidenced by the massive schism resulting in the so-called "Global Methodists."

congregations in his care: "We have spoken frankly to you Corinthians; our heart is wide open to you. There is no restriction in our affections but only in yours. In return—I speak as to children—open wide your hearts also."[2] (2 Cor. 6:11–12).

The Methodists seem to believe that we must work our way through open hearts and minds before we can have open doors. I can understand why they see it that way. It makes logical sense. If our hearts and minds are open, then we are more likely to have doors that swing wide open, physically and spiritually. However, more than one person has accused me of being a backwards thinker. Therefore, I harbor no reservations about reversing the order of the Methodist's motto so that it now reads: "Open doors. Open minds. Open hearts."

I want to start with open doors because this is the easiest of the three. Whether our hearts are in it or not, whether we are open-minded about strange and marginalized groups of people occupying our pews, we can physically unlock our doors and advertise it as a church that welcomes everyone. We can do everything that suggests we have an open-door policy without breaking much of a sweat. Sure, some of our folks might regret this policy on occasion, but overall, it is not too difficult for congregational leadership to push an open-door policy. It feels like the right thing to do.

We mainliners can maintain our tradition of an open table for communion even if we think and feel like slapping a few outreached hands that are grabbing for the wafer and miniature cup. We can officially become "Open and Affirming," to use a UCC catchphrase, even if very few of our people participate in a Pride parade or wear rainbow socks.[3] White and black congregations can create an alliance with their counterparts in the community, although most of their members may have never even worshiped with the "others". We can do all these things with very little, if any discomfort. We can have an open-door policy without investing much emotional or intellectual energy, without even having open hearts and open minds. And that's okay. This is a good first step because sometimes doing something whether our hearts and minds are in it or not can lead to a change of hearts and minds. I learned this from Aristotle, who suggested that virtues are found in humanity by doing the right actions.[4] Echoing

---

2. 2 Cor. 6:11–12.

3. "Open and Affirming" or "ONA" is the UCC's designation for a public welcome to the Rainbow Community.

4. This sentiment is expressed in his *Nicomachean Ethics, Book II*, ca. 350 BCE.

Evangelism

Aristotle, the American historian and philosopher, Will Durant, said that "we are what we repeatedly do."[5] Therefore, if we get into the habit of opening our doors and being a welcoming church, this will become who we are. It will inhabit, not inhibit, our thoughts and actions.

Working backwards from the Methodist motto, the next step after an open door is to have an open mind (which is in the second slot in both formulations of the motto). This has to do with being willing to listen and learn. It has to do with being willing to change our minds if the need arises. An open mind is a malleable mind. Most of us probably believe we have an open mind. I know I do. That's how I see myself, yet there is plenty of evidence to suggest that a mind that is truly open is rare. If our minds were like animal species, we would call the open mind an endangered species. Think about it: How many of us have ever changed our minds about anything of significance? When was the last time we did that?

Rather than sharing something about which I changed my mind (because I'm having a difficult time remembering something), I will tell you about the time I helped a couple of other people change *their* minds. This happened when I was the pastor at St. Andrew UCC in Louisville, Kentucky. We were working through the Open and Affirming discernment process. One of the more controversial discussions we had was about whether one's sexual orientation is a choice or an orientation. Most people by then had concluded it is *not* a choice for most people, but there were a few holdouts who were hanging on to that assumption.[6] Then, without any strategic forethought, I blurted out the question, "If you are straight, when did you decide to become straight?" For a few moments I could only hear crickets. A few weeks later, two men told me this question helped them change their minds about the topic. They now realize that no, people do not just wake up one morning and decide what their sexual orientation is.

Regrettably, the United Methodist Church has experienced denominational division, as holding an open mind does not necessarily result in consensus. Opening a mind is sometimes like trying to open a locked door with the wrong key. And yet, even that is not as difficult as having an open heart. Opening our hearts occurs at a much deeper level than opening our minds or doors. It gets to who we really are. We might be able to hide who

---

5. Durant, *The Story of Philosophy*, 87.

6. We need to remind ourselves that even if someone has made a free choice to be in same-sex relationships, their sexual orientation is not necessarily morally problematic. Most of the evidence suggests, however, that one does not simply choose their sexual orientation.

we are by opening our doors or engaging in an intellectual conversation about an important topic. We can do these things and convince ourselves and others that we are virtuous people with good values, people who follow Christ and love God and one another. On the surface, that's what it looks like we are doing when we open our doors and our minds. But opening our hearts is the most difficult of the three, which is why I think the Methodists should reverse the order of their motto and end with open hearts; the heart is the last of the three that will open. It might even take a spiritual crowbar.

OPEN EVANGELISM

In a post-Resurrection story from John 21, the disciples decide to try their hand at their former occupation—fishing. Unfortunately, their skills are now lacking. By daybreak they decide to give up and come back to shore emptyhanded, but as they are doing so, they see a man standing there rudely asking if they caught any fish. They answer in the negative, so he tells them to go back and cast their nets on the other side of the boat. I'm no professional fisherman, yet I can't imagine how that would make any difference. Strangely, they do not recognize that the man giving them an impromptu fishing lesson is Jesus himself, although there is a running theme in the post-Resurrection stories about Jesus being unrecognizable . . . until something happens. In this case, what happens is a net full of fish.

This story is almost cartoonish. When Simon Peter realizes that the resurrected Lord is the one who took these professional fishermen to school (pardon the fish pun), he decides to cover up his naked body with clothing and *then* jump into the water, an act that seems counterintuitive. Peter is obviously embarrassed, humiliated, and frazzled. Maybe that's why Jesus asks him three times, "Do you love me?" as they are later feasting on the fresh fish. This is a way to help Peter clean the slate after he had earlier denied knowing Jesus three times, and yet I think he also wants to make sure Peter has snapped out of his stupor.

Like all the fishing stories in the New Testament, there is a message or theme just under the surface (another pun; sorry). That theme is "evangelism". In the synoptic Gospels, when Jesus calls his first disciples, all fishermen, he tells them to drop their nets so they can become *fishers of people*, which is a great metaphor for evangelism. We are called to fish for people, these stories tell us, to cast our nets far and wide, nets that are woven from God's unconditional love and grace. We are called to lure people onto the

Sod of God (if I may change to a modern fishing analogy), not necessarily to our own congregations, although if the fish/people happen to land in our boats, no one's complaining.

Evangelism, also known as the "E" word, has a bit of a sordid (i.e., heavy) reputation in Christian history. From sword-wielding Crusaders to door-to-door white shirted young men to modern televangelism's prosperity message, evangelism has all too often been practiced by shady characters who use it for self-promotion and get-rich schemes. For these and other reasons, mainline Protestants often throw the baby out with the bathwater. Yes, the bathwater can get dirty and slimy, but the baby—evangelism—is worth cleaning up and saving.

What is needed is a fresh (i.e., lite) approach to evangelism, what I propose we call "open evangelism." We already practice an open table, accept all baptisms, and claim to have an open-door policy, so we might as well consider open evangelism. Here is how I define open evangelism: *To be open to fishing in ways we might not have considered before.* Open evangelism *is* casting our net on the other side of the boat. I can describe this in three ways:

1. It means opening ourselves *geographically*

   Technologically, we now have the capability to fish outside our local ponds. The pandemic years taught us, if not forced us, to move from "cane pole" evangelism to "wide net" evangelism, by taking advantage of our internet presence. Can we reach out to people who do not live in our geographical area? The once murky answer is now clearly "yes." Interestingly, televangelists have been doing this for years. Why not us?

2. It means opening ourselves *demographically*

   Are we always trying to catch the same fish from the same pond, or is there a little wiggle room here (yep, another pun)? I'm not just talking about *ethnic* demographics, although that is a good place to start because ethnic diversity is woefully absent in many American congregations. No matter how we envision this, casting our nets on the other side of the boat is a faithful way to fish for people.

3. It means opening ourselves *theologically*

   Here's where it might get tricky for some of us, where we might have a difficult time baiting our hooks. Historically, the bait we have used is "belief." Our belief systems are what we want people to nibble on and then take a bite. We dangle a shiny theological assertion in front of folks and ask them to take the bait. Then, if the fish "behaves" correctly (by not wiggling off the hook), they will "belong" . . . presumably in our boat.

As I suggested earlier, this is the order of traditional, or closed, evangelism, where the door and table are only open to those who are theologically like-minded. As I see it, however, asking folks to believe as we do at the outset of their faith journey can be problematic. People may not be ready for that yet. So, what would happen if we reversed the order? Maybe this should be our *line* (sorry again for the fish puns): "No matter who you are, where you are on life's journey, what you currently believe, or how well you behave, you belong here." No matter how we evangelize, let's admit one thing: there is nothing better than fresh fish.

PAUL THE SAINT VS. POPEYE THE SAILOR

Continuing with the fishing analogies, another principle in Christianity Lite is "Catch people wherever they are." For insight into this, let's turn to the wisdom (or not) of one of the greatest fishermen to ever "live": Popeye the Sailor.

There is an old comic strip where a giant octopus has Olive Oyl in its grasp and Popeye is standing helpless on a nearby boat, saying, "Of all the things, why did I give up spinach for Lent." Popeye is such a well-known figure in our culture that I don't even need to explain that. He is also a philosopher of sorts. When Popeye says, "I am what I am, and that's all that I am" (pronounced "I yam what I yam, and that's all that I yam") he is either lying to himself or to us. Most of us tend to think that he is always "what I yam."

But the portrayal of *Popeye* was not always consistent. For example, in his debut storyline on January 17, 1929, Popeye's superhuman strength stems from the "luck" he acquires by rubbing the feathers of the head of Bernice, a "whiffle" or white hen. In that first story, he is "lucky" enough to survive fifteen gunshot wounds, a scene that would not be printable today considering America's gun violence epidemic. By the end of 1929, Popeye's strength and endurance had become a regular fixture of his character, but it wasn't until 1932 that *spinach* becomes the primary source of his strength and endurance. Speaking of how flexible his character is, here's a quote from Popeye's Wikipedia page: "Popeye seems bereft of manners and uneducated, yet he often comes up with solutions to problems that seem insurmountable to the police or the scientific community. He has displayed Sherlock Holmes-like investigative prowess, scientific ingenuity, and successful diplomatic arguments."[7]

Does that sound like someone that can humbly claim, "I yam what I yam, and that's all that I yam"? Even his pipe cannot claim to be a single-purpose pipe. It is highly versatile, serving at various times as a cutting torch, jet engine, propeller, periscope, musical instrument, and a whistle with which he produces his trademark "toot". He also eats spinach through his pipe, sometimes sucking in the can along with the contents. And then there are the alternative lyrics applied to the song, "Popeye the Sailor," a song about him eating worms, spitting out the germs, and living in a garbage can.

Despite all this, most people see Popeye as "I yam what I yam, and that's all that I yam," namely, a one-eyed squinting sailor with massive forearms, a speech impediment with bad grammar, and a love for spinach and Olive Oyl.[8] Popeye is a hero *because* of his consistency. He is a role model for those who aspire to be steady, unchanging, stable, reliable, and trustworthy. Consistency is obviously a trait that lends itself to trustworthiness. Our reliability gives our Christian witness credibility. We hope that everyone experiences us in pretty much the same way, a way that creates trust in the Gospel we espouse. We want to become the same person to all people to represent Christ in an effective manner. We want to have consistency in character, stability in spirituality, and reliability in our religious faith because without some sense of coherence, no one would believe anything we have to say. Popeye the sailor's philosophy is that we should be an open book to people, as much as we can be.

However, sometimes we might have to become someone we are not—at least not yet. Sometimes we might need to gently close our open book, at least for the moment, and be open to who other people need us to be.

---

7. Wikipedia, "Popeye."

8. The girl, not the actual oil. Also, does his name, "Popeye," suggest that one of his eyes had popped out, thus explaining his constant squint?

Sometimes our Popeye the Sailor side needs to go swab the deck and allow our Paul the Saint side to take over the helm. Paul the Apostle, formerly known as Saul, transforms his life from a violent persecutor of the church to its greatest defender. He is the most influential missionary of the first century, doing more to bring the Christian faith to the gentiles than any other person in history. His approach, articulated in 1 Corinthians 9:22, is simple: "I have become all things to all people, that I might by all means save some." Paul uses the word "win" all throughout this chapter, not in a competitive way, but more in the way of Dale Carnegie's "How to *Win* Friends and Influence People." He's talking about winning people over to the fellowship of Christ, including (in his time and place) traditional Jews who are focused on the Law of Moses *and* gentiles who are, for lack of a better word, pagans.

Paul knows he can't fully express the same side of himself to both groups. Rather than swallow his spinach and win people through strength and the sheer force of his personality, Paul swallows his ego to win people to Christ through love, sensitivity, and vulnerability. He teaches us that sometimes we need to be "Wimpy." Paul's approach compels us to find compatibility and commonality with others. This requires us to relate to people where they are, to put ourselves in other's shoes and walk a mile in their moccasins.

There is an added benefit to this: When we become all things to all people, we also benefit from others, who become all things to us. I call this the "clean little secret" of sharing our faith with others. To be an effective *witness* requires "*with-ness*". So, yes, it is true: I yam what I yam, and that's all that I yam. We are encouraged to be authentic, steady, and consistent followers of Christ. At the same time, I yam all things to all people, that I might save some. We are also called to be adaptable, flexible, and changeable.

Who is right? Popeye the Sailor or Paul the Saint? Who has the best approach? "I am what I am" authenticity, or "I am all things to all people" adaptability? My answer to that question is "yes." We are called to do both. This is a paradox in terms of the Christian witness. We are called to be an open book to people, knowing that sometimes we need to turn the page. Even so, we should always—always—eat our spinach.

12

Eschatology

UTOPIANISM

HEAVY-HANDED CHRISTIANITY SEEKS UTOPIANISM (according to their understanding of utopia), whereas Christianity Lite takes a more practical approach and seeks improvement in the here and now, which is more flexible and adjustable. Utopianism or perfectionism is difficult to ignore, however.

One of the roads I have traversed many times is I-64 from St. Louis, Missouri to Louisville, Kentucky. About halfway between, near Evansville, Indiana is a little community called New Harmony. It was founded in 1814 on the banks of the Wabash River as a spiritual sanctuary by a group of eight hundred pious Germans. They believed the Second Coming of Christ was imminent, so they pursued Christian "perfection" through every aspect of their daily conduct. They were trying to create a utopia. Unfortunately, their little community didn't last long. By March 1827, the utopian experiment had failed, plagued by disputes over scripture and constant quarreling. That's not surprising, is it? Today, if you go to New Harmony, you can visit some interesting historical sites, take in some beautiful scenery, and go visit Paul Tillich's memorial. Tillich was a twentieth-century German theologian who migrated to the United States in 1933 after the Nazis censured some of his writings. Later, he discovered New Harmony and was so taken by it that he visited often and wrote many of his important works there. His ashes were even interred there after he died in 1965.[1]

Despite being a beautiful scenic environment for one of the greatest theologians in history, New Harmony did not live up to its original

---

1. "New Harmony, Indiana, Wikipedia, http://en.m.wikipedia.org.

expectations. Every attempt to create a utopian or "perfect" society has failed because, well, people are people. And yet, we can't help but wonder what a perfect society or world would look like. We know that will never happen, so when people say, "Well, in a perfect world . . ." what they are really saying is yes, this or that should happen, but we know it won't.

In John Lennon's popular song, "Imagine," he envisions a world that would be perfect (from his perspective).² In Lennon's utopia there is no heaven or hell, or even religion (which I can partly understand, although if that happened, I would be unemployed, so I'm not on board with that just yet). In his imagination, people are "livin' for today," which is the kind of carefree attitude that befits a rock star's privileged existence. There are no countries, nothing to kill or die for, and so everyone is "livin' in peace." Sounding even more idealistic, he imagines a world with no possessions, no greed or hunger, and all things are shared (which begs the question, if we have no possessions, then what will we be sharing?). Finally, he dreams that "the world will live as one." (I'm sure that phrase struck a nerve with folks who fear the possibility of a "one-world government.")

Lennon's song, while easy on the ears, is just never going to happen. It is easy to dismiss his song as the product of an overactive imagination of a famous rock star who spent most of his later years in an isolated bubble with Yoko Ono. As we know, his world didn't end very peacefully either. The hard to swallow truth is that humanity will never ever reinvent the Garden of Eden. It's just not going to happen. We can only do our best in our little corner of the world to make it a better place to live. As Sir Robert Baden-Powell, the founder of the Boy Scouts, is often quoted as saying, "Try to leave this world a little better than you found it."³

If the biblical writers had a list of motives for writing what they did, creating a more perfect world might be at the top of that list. The New Testament phrase for this is "the Kingdom of God," which is what, exactly? The New Testament scholar, John Dominic Crossan, famously said, "The Kingdom of God is what the world would be if God were directly and immediately in charge."⁴ That quote has fascinated me for years. What *would* the world be like if God were directly and immediately in charge? Would

---

2. Lennon, "Imagine." These lyrics sparked controversy and led to the song being banned from some radio stations after 9/11. http://www.abc.net.au.

3. Wikipedia "Leaving the World a Better Place," This is also called the "campsite" or "campground" rule.

4. Crossan, *Jesus*, 55.

it not be more perfect? In the book of Revelation, the writer is so invested in a more perfect world that he suggests it will only happen when God hits the reset button: "Then I saw a new heaven and a new earth, for the first heaven and the first earth had passed away."[5] Let's just start over, he is saying. Yet how is this new universe—heaven and earth—more perfect? For starters, "the sea (is) no more." Don't panic, seafood lovers, because the "sea" is Bible-speak for *chaos*. Can we imagine a world with no chaos? That would be more perfect, wouldn't it?

In this new world, symbolized by a New Jerusalem, God dwells among the people—directly and immediately in charge. Because of that there are no more tears—nothing to cry about—no more death in fact. Was the writer a little too idealistic about how the world could be? Yes, but if we step back and not take him so literally, what we see is a writer who just wants to make the world a better place to live; not a perfect world, just one that is improving. Perfection is a mountain whose summit we will never reach, and yet the biblical writers, Jesus, 19th century German pietists, Paul Tillich, John Lennon, Sir Robert Baden-Powell, John Dominic Crossan, and a host of other folks we never heard of, are telling us that we don't have to move to New Harmony, Indiana to make some improvements.

JUDGING LIVESTOCK

The parable of the sheep and goats in Matthew 25:31–46 sounds like something that might take place at a livestock show. All that's missing is a rodeo. The Son of Man is the livestock judge, and we are the animals. I don't know much about livestock judging, but it seems like an art form as much as a science. As far as I know, stock shows are never mentioned in the Bible. Archaeologists have yet to discover the ancient ruins of rodeo arenas, but there is no doubt that the people have a great amount of knowledge about domestic animals, particularly sheep. In the ancient Near East, including Israel, shepherding was a common occupation. It plays an outsized role in the biblical story, from Moses and David, who were both shepherds, to Jesus, the Good Shepherd who also becomes known as the sacrificial lamb. Even today, pastors are known as shepherds.

To refer to someone or a group of people as "sheep" is derogatory these days, but biblically speaking, being counted among God's sheep is a good thing. The biblical writers utilized images with which they were

5. Rev. 21:1.

most familiar, and there were a lot of sheep and shepherds running around, grazing in green pastures and chilling beside still waters. The Israelites were sheep experts. The art of livestock judging came naturally for them. Because of that, *people judging sheep* became a metaphor for *God judging people* in the biblical literature. Jesus's parable about the Son of Man judging people is analogous to a rancher judging or analyzing the quality of his or her cattle. Here is my reimagining of the parable of the sheep and goats:

A small-time rancher is trying to make a decent living in the "gig economy."[6] One of his favorite gigs is livestock judging. The annual stock show has come to town, so he drives to the venue, parks his truck and walks to the large building where the stock show is taking place. He has been selected to be a judge because of his expertise. He quickly finds his judge's chair, surrounded by his competent assistants, and announces that he is ready. He has prepared for a difficult and exacting day. He has some guidelines to help him judge the livestock, but he knows that sometimes the differences are so subtle it takes an extremely keen eye to see them. On this day, however, he notices that there are two species of domestic animals brought before him: sheep and goats. He asks the stock show officials what this means. They tell him that all he needs to do is separate the sheep from the goats. With a confused look on his face, he obliges. He judges the animals and then he goes home, telling his wife that he just got paid for the easiest gig of his life. It's not that difficult separating sheep from goats.

Likewise, judging people is the easiest gig in God's job description. It's not as subjective as we might think. It's not an art form. It's not a guessing game. It's as easy as distinguishing black from white. According to God's guidelines for judging, the sheep are the ones who feed the hungry, give drink to the thirsty, welcome the stranger, clothe the naked, take care of the sick, and visit those in prison. The goats are the ones who do not do those things.

This parable is both terrifying and reassuring. It is terrifying and oppressive to those who do not meet the standards set forth in the guidelines, yet reassuring to those who do. We tend to think God judges us in one of two ways, if God judges us at all. We tend to think God judges us based on the quality of our faith or the quantity of our beliefs, but this parable upsets the applecart of traditional heavy-handed and impractical theologizing.

---

6. The gig economy is the economic system in which a workforce of people engages in freelance and/or side-employment. It is also a perfect way to describe people who graduate from Texas A & M with an agricultural degree. "Aggies," as they are called, use a thumbs-up gesture when they say "Gig 'em" to intimidate athletic rivals.

ESCHATOLOGY

It takes a very different approach. Here Jesus suggests that God judges us based not on faith or beliefs, but on what we do; specifically, how we treat the least of these, the neediest, the most vulnerable people in our midst. This is terrifying because I certainly don't spend all my time doing those things. I will never be a grand champion in God's stock show. Because of that, this parable concerns me. At the same time, the parable is reassuring because at least I know what the judge is judging.

13

Sin

FALL UPWARD

TRADITIONAL CHRISTIANITY EXPLAINS THE presence of sin as a problem in search of a convenient solution. The solution is salvation, which only the church can offer (it claims). Christianity Lite sees the role of sin in human history in a very different light: as the result of an awakened conscience. Sin entered the world when humanity developed a conscience, shed their moral ignorance, and became culpable. Sin, then, is an evolutionary step forward. Since we are too close and too indoctrinated about sin to garner a unique perspective, maybe we need a fresh perspective from someone less affected by our history and tradition, such as aliens from another planet.

If aliens spy on us in church someday, they might wonder why Christians do certain things, like splash babies on the top of their heads, eat tasteless wafers, drink only a single sip of wine, and talk to an invisible person named Jesus. Singing might be a weird concept to aliens. Imagine what they might think if they spy on a Pentecostal worship service with dancing and tongue talking. If the aliens hang around our worship services long enough to learn our language, they will begin to pick up on some things said or sung that might seem odd, strange, peculiar, or mysterious to them. The concept of sin, however, might be the most puzzling of all.

Sin is a mystery. What is it exactly? What does it look like? Is it a particular type of act, or is it a state of being? Where did it come from? Are we born *in* sin, or do we learn *to* sin? Is nature or nurture responsible for our sinfulness, or is it the result of free will? The aliens would not be the first to ponder these questions. Our ancestors have been thinking about this for a very long time. The ancient Hebrews, for example, came up with an origin

Sin

story to explain the mystery of sin. Their unraveling of this mystery begins in the book of Genesis where God places the first human being in a garden, to "till it and keep it."[1] Notice this story implies that sin entered the world when there was agriculture, which didn't occur until about twelve thousand years ago. Before that, human beings were nomadic hunter-gatherers. This begs the question: Didn't the hunter-gatherer sin with as much gusto as the gardener and farmer? I have it on good authority that there was such a problem with random or vengeful spearing among the hunters that a group of "spear control" activists raised a big stink about it.

According to sin's origin story, the Lord God gave some odd instructions to the first man: "You may freely eat of every tree of the garden, but of the tree of the knowledge of good and evil you shall not eat, for in the day that you eat of it you shall die."[2] A lot of ink has been spilled attempting to explain why God wouldn't want the first man to eat of that tree and develop a moral compass or conscience. My best guess is that God had a much easier job when human beings remained in a state of innocence.

Scientists give us a complementary (and more believable) theory. They say we were barely a knuckle-dragging ancestor away from being wild animals ourselves when we began to develop the ability to discern between good and evil, which also implies an earlier state of innocence. Animals, of course, do a lot of things that we would consider sinful behavior on the part of humanity, but we don't refer to their behavior as sin. That word doesn't apply to them at all. There is bad behavior all over the place. Nature is "red in tooth and claw" as Tennyson says, bloody and violent, and yet there is no sin.[3]

The Apostle Paul explains it this way: "Sin was indeed in the world before the law (the Law of Moses, which is rooted in the knowledge of good and evil), but sin is not *reckoned* when there is no law." Animals are not bound by any laws (not even "leash laws"—pet owners get fined for that), so sin is not reckoned to them. Here's some interesting irony: After a woman is created to be the man's companion (and to take the blame for what happens, no doubt), an *animal*, namely a serpent, tempts the woman to take the first bite from the fruit of that tree. The fruit is unnamed. Let's not give apples any more credit or blame for opening humanity's eyes. They already get the credit for keeping the doctor away. The serpent is unnamed as well.

1. Gen. 2:15.
2. Gen. 2:16–17.
3. Tennyson, "In Memoriam A.H.H."

It is not the devil or Satan (as is often assumed). The serpent is a crafty wild animal that no one wants to encounter in a garden. The serpent is *amoral* (without a moral compass) and feels no remorse for tempting the innocent woman to take a disobedient bite.

Here's something else we often miss about this story: The first humans broke *the very first law*. The. Very. First. Law. It's like a child unwrapping their first ever Christmas present and *breaking it* before they ever get to play with it. And then the parents kick the child out of the house. From this story we get the doctrine of "original sin," which is rooted in the words of the Apostle Paul: "Just as sin came into the world through one man, and death came through sin, and so death *spread to all* (like a virus) because all have sinned."[4] Notice that Paul blames the man rather than the woman, proving that Paul was less sexist than some have suggested.

Biblically speaking, the original sin was taking a bite out of a forbidden fruit that led to greater awareness of wrongdoing (and nakedness). Historically speaking, the original sin might have been the first time a caveman clobbered a cavewoman with a club and realized that physical abuse is a terrible idea. Whatever the original sin was, it seems to have infected us *like a virus*. Or has it affected us *like a vaccine?*

Traditionally, theologians describe the event that took place in the Garden of Eden as "the Fall of Man," the heaviest doctrine in the Judeo-Christian tradition.[5] By using the word "fall," traditionalists characterize it as a fall *downward*, as if humanity took a step *down* from God's purposes for humanity when they yanked that fruit from that tree branch and took a big juicy bite. Allow me to offer a different perspective. I suggest the Fall of Humanity was a fall *upward*. The Franciscan priest, Richard Rohr, is one of the most prominent supporters of this view. In his book, *Falling Upward*, he writes this: "Yes, they (Adam and Eve) 'sinned' and were cast out of the Garden of Eden, but from those very acts came 'consciousness,' conscience, and their own further journey. But all started with transgression."[6] "Falling down and moving up," he continues, "is, in fact, the most counterintuitive message in most of the world's religions, including and most especially Christianity. We grow spiritually much more by doing it wrong than by doing it right. That might just be the central message of how spiritual growth

---

4. Rom. 5:12.

5. And you know what they say, "The heavier they are, the harder they fall," or something like that.

6. Rohr, *Falling Upward*, xx.

happens . . . I think it is the only workable meaning of any remaining notion of 'original sin.'"⁷

The Fall of Humanity was a fall upward. If the original sin infected us like a virus, then the *awareness* of our sinfulness has become our vaccine. What was Jesus doing for forty days and nights in the wilderness as he was being tempted by the devil? He was getting inoculated, immunized, and vaccinated against the virus of sin. I will give the same advice I gave my parishioners during the height of the pandemic: Get the damn shot!

GETTING OFF THE HOOK

The French philosopher, Voltaire, declared that his life was a struggle. Evil and suffering in the world might have had something to do with that. The spiritual struggle is real, but it might not always be what we think it is. I like to compare us to a fish on a hook struggling to be free. Like fish, rather than trying to keep our heads *above* water, we spend most of our time struggling to keep our heads *underwater*, in the spiritual environment to which we are accustomed. The fish on a hook analogy is a great way to describe how we respond to God's *lure* of love. God is trying to lure us toward the Sod of God.

Like a fish resisting being jerked out of the water onto dry land, God's lure of love seems too drastic, too impractical, and too unfamiliar. We don't want to go there, so we do everything we can to keep from being reeled in. The word "struggle" means "to make forceful or violent efforts to get free of restraint or constriction," just like a fish on a hook. Our struggle might not always seem so dramatic. We might not create a big splash trying to break free from God's lure of love. Still, no matter how forceful or violent we are or aren't, we *are* struggling to get off the hook, even if we are just gently pulling against whatever is on the other end of the line. We *are* struggling to stay where we are. We are struggling against spiritual progress, whether we know it or not. We are struggling to maintain the status quo, to stay in our comfort zones. It is easier to breathe when we are doing what comes natural to us.

But there is a catch—pardon the pun. While you and I struggle against being yanked out of our spiritual comfort zones, we are, *at the same time*, desiring that God's love lures us onto God's Sod. Yet we know that being reeled onto the Sod of God means getting pulled out of our comfort zones,

---

7. Ibid, xxii.

our natural spiritual habitat, and this creates a tension within us. "Should I stay, or should I go?" asks the British punk rock band, The Clash.[8]

The Apostle Paul hits the nail on the head when he describes his own struggle to live in the Sod of God. In Romans 7:15 he famously writes, "I do not understand my own actions. For I do not do what I want, but I do the very thing I hate." He wants to allow God to reel him in, yet he still finds himself struggling against it, and he doesn't know why. There is a powerful pull within us. Paul names this the "sin that dwells within me."[9] Sinfulness is our natural habitat. We are born into it. Literally speaking, we are born struggling to stay in the water of the womb, where it is nice, cozy, and comfortable. We must be pushed out, pulled out, or even cut out, kicking and screaming, and once we are out, we become even more resistant to the lure of God's love.

We spend the rest of our lives struggling, scuffling, sparring, and scrapping against landing on the Sod of God because it doesn't seem like a natural place for us. It feels like we are swimming in uncharted waters or worse, we fear flopping around on dry land. We fear that too much spiritual stimulation and growth is like being a fish out of water. Paul doubles down on his view of human nature by saying, "For I do not do the good I want, but the evil I do not want is what I do."[10] Paul feels the tension of a man who is being lured by God's love but continues to struggle against it. It is a monumental struggle. Have you ever tried to pull an alligator gar out of the water? I hear they put up a ferocious fight. That's like how Paul describes his spiritual struggle. It is a ferocious fight. He refers to himself as "wretched" and in need of rescuing.[11] He is drowning in his sin, and he knows it, but like us he really doesn't want to come out of the water. Drowning or not, it's where we are most comfortable.

One of the greatest lies we tell ourselves is that we are struggling *against* our sinful nature. For the most part, we are not. For the most part our sinful nature—our human nature—is struggling against our holy nature, made in the image of God. We might think we are fighting against the pull of our sinful nature, but the truth is, like a fish with a hook in its mouth, we are most likely fighting against the pull of God's lure of love. The struggle is not to get out, as the orthodox claim; *the struggle is to stay in.*

8. The Clash, "Should I Stay, or Should I Go."
9. Rom. 7:17.
10. Rom. 7:19.
11. Rom. 7:24.

When I was a youngster, I did a fair amount of fishing. My favorite memory is going fishing with my great-grandmother Ward. She was already in her 90s. She was old school. She would sit on the bank of the Concho River in a tattered old lawn chair, with multiple lines cast into the river, fishing for catfish. She wore a bonnet to protect her face from the sun, and a crusty old spittoon sat on the ground beside her. She was surprisingly accurate at spitting. Suddenly, one of her rods would bend and I would hear her ancient voice creaking out the words, "Jimmy, I've got a bite!" I'd stop everything to help her reel it in. The struggle of a catfish was too much for great-grandma Ward.

Likewise, the struggle for us is real. Even if we are somewhat serious about our so-called spiritual journey, we are pulling against the One who is trying to lure us in. Sometimes we even find a way to get off the hook. Thankfully, God is a good fisherperson. God will cast multiple divine lines into the waters of sin, sickness, and sadness until each one of us are brought to the shores of the Sod of God, kicking and screaming, or rather flapping and flopping.

COVER STORY

I imagine the process of determining what a cover story will be for a monthly magazine or a headline for a daily newspaper is interesting work. One of the few magazines I subscribe to is *Texas Monthly*. In their November 2024 edition, the cover features a strange looking taco with the words "Republic of Tacos." The title of the related article in the magazine is "The 50 Best Tacos in Texas." (I would love to have been the researcher for that article.) In the December edition of *Texas Monthly* the front cover is a picture of a Texas Longhorn with the caption, "Longer than Ever." The article inside talks about the origin of the Longhorn and the fact that they are being bred these days for record-setting horns (which seems a little cruel to me).[12]

One of the questions I have been asking myself for decades is, "What is it that separates us from the rest of the animals?" There are many good answers to that question, but here's one that comes to mind: Human beings are *storytellers*. We all have stories to tell, although some of us are better at telling them than others. I am reminded of the late Jimmy Buffett's song, *That's My Story and I'm Stickin' to it*. Buffett's playful and lighthearted song

---

12. Can we think of anything more Texan than tacos and Longhorns? Aggie fans might not agree.

is about the art of storytelling and maintaining one's personal narrative, no matter how outlandish it may seem.[13]

It is important to tell our stories. We should find a way—even a small way—to share our experiences, memories, thoughts, and dreams with our loved ones. For Father's Day in 2024, my oldest daughter, Christen, decided she wants me to share my story, so she found an online company that sends one question per week to my email inbox. I answer it with approximately a one-page essay, and then at the end of a certain amount of time the company will publish all my essays in book form. At the end of this project I will have written a brief memoir, and I've already started thinking about what the cover story might be if they ask me: "Accidental Preacher"—because, as I explained at the outset of this book, I sort of got into the ministry by accident.

A cover story is usually defined as the featured article in a magazine, yet there are other kinds of cover stories. A cover story can also be "a story made up to disguise one's identity or activity."[14] In other words, a cover story can be a story that provides *cover*. This is the stuff that makes for a good spy novel.

Other than the cover story for magazines and for people who are hiding their identities, there is a third way to understand a cover story. It could be a story that covers all of our other stories. It could be the story that stands above everything else about us, that affects everything about us. We might call this our "meta-story" or, as the Canadian journalist Malcolm Gladwell calls it, our "over-story." Think of a tall tree that serves as a canopy for the ground below, offering shade, protection, and maybe even nourishment for everything underneath it.[15]

What is our cover story, the story that stands over everything else about us? One possible answer for many of my readers is *the Gospel story*, the good news or good story about Jesus. As Christians, shouldn't the Gospel overshadow everything else about us? Shouldn't it be our cover story? Like a heavy blanket on a cold winter night, the Gospel provides cover for our stories. It doesn't conceal or cover up who we are, but it does change how comfortable we are with ourselves. Let me offer three examples of the Gospel's cover story, juxtaposed with our story.

---

13. "That's My Story and I'm Stickin' to it," by Jimmy Buffett, on his album *Off to See the Lizard*, MCA, 1989.

14. "Cover story," Collins (noun), http://www.collinsdictionary.com.

15. Gladwell, *Revenge of the Tipping Point*, 51–52.

Sin

1. Our story: We are fallen and fallible, corruptible and contemptible hypocritical sinners.

    In Romans 7:15, the Apostle Paul said that we do not do what we want, instead we do the very thing we hate. Because of that, we are not comfortable with ourselves. That's our story until we apply the cover story of the Gospel, which Paul sums up a few verses later: "Therefore there is now no condemnation for those who are in Christ Jesus."[16] The good news of Jesus Christ is our cover story. In fact, one (morbid sounding) interpretation of the Gospel is that the blood of Jesus *covers* our sins. The Gospel is our story, and we're sticking to it.

2. Our story: We are perishable, dishonorable, weak, physical human beings.

    We are mortal. This is our story, although when we apply the cover story of the Gospel, specifically the Resurrection story, our story changes. Reflecting on how our story has changed, the Apostle Paul recorded these words in 1 Corinthians 15:42f: "So it is with the resurrection of the dead. What is sown is perishable; what is raised is imperishable. It is sown in dishonor; it is raised in glory. It is sown in weakness; it is raised in power. It is sown a physical body; it is raised a spiritual body." This is now our story, and we're sticking to it as well.

3. Our story: We are part of a world with imperfect and unjust leaders, rulers, and governments, including our own.

    We are citizens of kingdoms, democracies, and everything in between, and none of them have ever succeeded in creating a perfect society. This is our story, whether we are Americans or Armenians, Germans or Jamaicans. Nevertheless, when we apply the cover story of the Gospel our story changes. We become first and foremost citizens of a righteous realm, a sacred society, a divine democracy, the Kingdom of God.

We see this cover story in John 18, where Pontius Pilate, the unjust governor of the Roman province of Judea, asks Jesus at his kangaroo trial, "Are you the King of the Jews?"[17] Pilate assumes that Jesus wants to dethrone Herod and become the next Jewish puppet-king for Rome. At the

---

16. Rom. 8:1.
17. Jn. 18:34.

time, Jesus's followers are hoping for the same. They believe the solution to their problems is someone else perched on the thrones in Jerusalem and in Rome. They want Jesus to be a "messiah-king," which was the most common way to define a messiah in that place and time. To everyone's surprise, however, including Pilate's, Jesus says, "My Kingdom does not belong to this world . . . my Kingdom is not from here."[18] This is a challenge to our identity; it has the potential to change our story. We tend to see ourselves as citizens of nation states first, but when the Gospel becomes our cover story, we are challenged to see ourselves as citizens of the Kingdom of God first. Unfortunately, two thousand years after Jesus gave us this cover story, we still tend to "kick off the covers" like we would a heavy blanket in bed. We still prefer our *heavier* cover stories.

---

18. Jn. 18:36.

14

Grace

GRACE ON THE PLATE, IN THE HOUSE, IN THE CAR, AND IN THE STATS

I'M A GRACE MAN; I make no bones about it. Although it is perhaps the most difficult of all the so-called Christian doctrines in terms of understanding it and practicing it, I am drawn to its promise to help us progress beyond the heavy-handed, overwhelming, judgmental, manipulative, narrowly defined Christian tradition to which we have grown far too accustomed. I won't attempt to draw hard conclusions about the doctrine of grace in this essay—because that would nullify what grace is or might be. Instead, I will just share a few of my thoughts about grace that have sprouted up in my mind in surprisingly inexplicable yet rewarding ways over the years.

My first thought is that grace is the *lightest* of all the doctrines that have spiced up our Intro to Theology textbooks. It is lite on its feet. It is applicable in all situations or contexts. Grace "spreads" smoothly over our theology and devotional material. It is the "gravy" of Christian theology. God's grace is poured on us like gravy poured on a plateful of Thanksgiving fare. This suggests that grace should be the heaviest of all doctrines, and yet it makes everything lite.

My second thought is that grace is the most *convenient* of all the doctrines in the pantheon of Christian theology. It is ready and available to overshadow almost everything else about our faith, much like the roofs that cover our homes. Grace is a multipurpose doctrine. A great example of this was proposed by John Wesley, one of the founders of Methodism.[1] He theorized that grace consists of three aspects or stages:

1. Prevenient Grace

   Prevenient grace is operative before we are even aware of God's love and grace. Using a house as an analogy for the Kingdom of God, prevenient grace is located on the front yard or front porch, before the person even considers walking through the front door. One day a person is playing in the yard and an event occurs that makes them curious about what is inside the house, so they walk to the front door and knock.

2. Justifying Grace

   Justifying grace is the grace that initially, if not primitively and naively brings us through the front door into the Kingdom of God. This is the season in a person's life when the love of God becomes "real," either experientially or as one imagines it. This is the crossing of the threshold into a new life, a new purpose, a new calling.

3. Sanctifying Grace

   Sanctifying grace is the grace that helps us grow in faith and spirituality as we "dwell in the house of the Lord our whole life long."[2] It is the grace that operates inside the house, even as it prepares us to go outside and play with those that are covered under the umbrella of God's prevenient grace.

A critic might call this a theory of *convenient* grace. We can also call it *layered* grace. Like gravy, it covers every stage of our faith development.

Similarly, my third thought about grace is that it works from *afar*. Our distance from "God stuff" like faith, spirituality, church, etc. is largely irrelevant. Grace doesn't care how far away we are from where we need to be. On my best days I follow Jesus like an undercover cop follows a perp. I park my car about a block down the street from Jesus' house, waiting for him to come outside. When he does, he hops in his car and goes out into the world. I follow him, but I keep a safe distance. He knows it. He sees me

---

1. For a thorough review of this, see Carder, "A Wesleyan Understanding of Grace."
2. Ps. 23:6b.

back there, trailing him, but he still loves and accepts me anyway, which is what we mean by the word "grace".

My fourth thought about grace is that it doesn't include any *asterisks*. In my view, there is a difference between those who understand God's grace to be accompanied by asterisks (grace with caveats or conditions), and those who understand God's grace to be without any asterisks (unconditional).[3] If we want to advance the cause of Christ in a lasting, transformative way, then let's shed the asterisk. This isn't baseball.

GRACE AT THE CARD TABLE

Imagine you are sitting down across a card table from Jesus. Fortunately, the game you are playing is not competitive. It's not a zero-sum game, a game where someone must win and someone must lose. Instead, the object of the game is for you to play a card that will require Jesus to play the Grace card in response. "Grace" is defined as God's unconditional, unmerited, and unearned love, mercy, and forgiveness. Grace is God's "ace in the hole." It's God's trump card, because it trumps anything we might think, say, or do. If God has a card up the divine sleeve, it's the Grace card.

You, however, are dealt five cards for your hand and you need to decide *which* card to play so that Jesus will be obliged to play the Grace card. Do you play the Sacrifice card, the Law of Moses card, the Good Works card, the Faith card, or the Belief card? Which card do you need to play to win or earn God's grace? Some of those cards sound very Old Testament to you, but you remember what you learned in Sunday school, that for the ancient Israelites, the sacrificial system and the Law of Moses were super important to them. Once upon a time, these were thought to be the best cards for God's people to play.

Take Abram and Sarai, for instance. Eventually, these two lovebirds would be renamed "Abraham and Sarah," which means they probably didn't even have to change the names on their birth certificates or drivers' licenses. No need to go through all that government red tape. They were just a couple of elderly people with no special purpose in life until the Lord showed up and told them to pack their bags and move to another place, the Land of Canaan. This was a dicey journey because the Land of Canaan was full of, well, Canaanites. Since the Lord specifically asked Abram and Sarai to move to a more promising location, they must have thought they

---

3. For an overview of the doctrine of grace, see Gulley, *If Grace Is True*.

were already recipients of God's unconditional love and grace. Nevertheless, Abram does what people often did in the ancient world before their religious systems had fully developed and when there were no buildings in which to worship their god or gods: they built *altars*. And what did they do on top of those altars? *They offered burnt sacrifices.*

We still have altars today, but most of us do not use them as butcher tables or vegetable stands. We don't ritualistically slaughter animals—much less our first-born children, which was a thing back in the day. Nor do we bring in the first fruits from our gardens or crops, start a fire, and then offer them as a smoky, yet pleasing fragrance to God. Still, people thought they could procure God's grace or favor by playing the Sacrifice card on makeshift altars, and then later, during and after King Solomon's time, on the official altar in the Temple in Jerusalem. This was the card they played, hoping God would find that acceptable. Instead, the biblical writers make it clear that God desires "mercy, not sacrifice."[4] Jesus makes this even clearer in his response to the Pharisees who were criticizing him for dining with tax collectors and sinners. Rather than showing mercy to sinners, they believed he should be bringing sacrificial offerings to the Temple. Jesus thought otherwise.[5]

When Moses came along a few hundred years after Abraham and long before Solomon's temple was built, he got the idea that what people need to do to win God's grace is to follow a very specific set of laws. This was a very practical idea for a nation still in its infancy, a nation trying to become more civilized, stable, and religiously consistent. As Israel developed into a nation, the people began to play the Law of Moses card as much as they could. They hoped God would then play the Grace card on their behalf. It was a good try, but the problem with the Law is that no one could follow it without goofing up. "Goofing up" is my terminology for "sin." Centuries later, one such person who tries hard to follow the Law's every jot and tittle is a man named Saul, who, after he saw the (blinding) light of Christ, is renamed "Paul". Paul concludes that the only possible outcome following the Law to win God's approval is God's "tsk-tsk".[6]

Whether God ever plays the tsk-tsk card or not—a very debatable topic—as Christians we have been taught that neither the Sacrifice card nor the Law of Moses card is a good play. Sacrifices are empty rituals (unless the

4. Hos. 6:6.
5. Mt. 9:10–13.
6. Gal. 2:15–21.

Grace

"cooked" food is available to eat). And relying upon complete adherence to a set of laws to curry God's favor will one day expose us for what we truly are: People who goof up.

After a moment of clarity, you discard those two cards and look at the next card in your deck, the Good Works card. You think to yourself that maybe this will get Jesus to play the Grace card in response. The Good Works card seems like a safe choice. It is always a favorite among the unchurched and the under-churched. It is a secular rather than sacred card, yet it still seems like a practical choice to make if we want to obtain God's grace. Unlike the Sacrifice and Law of Moses cards, the Good Works card is not specific. It doesn't tell us to sacrifice animals. It doesn't give us a list of six hundred and thirteen commandments as does the Law of Moses, some of which make no sense for us today. The non-specific requirement of the Good Works card is its strength, but it is also its weakness. It is too vague to be of much value. Yes, we should be "good," but how does one define "good"? How good do we need to be for Jesus to feel obliged to play the Grace card?

You look up momentarily from your hand of cards at Jesus, who is sitting there smiling and waiting for you to make a play. Still feeling pressure to play the right card, you look at the final two cards, the Faith card and the Belief card. This feels a little more "New Testament-like." Surely one of these will get Jesus to play the Grace card!

The Apostle Paul was very much a Faith card guy. He even proposes the theory that Abraham won God's grace through his faith rather than through sacrificial rituals. The Law of Moses developed after Abraham, of course, so that wasn't even a choice for him. Paul writes in Romans 4:13, "For the promise that (Abraham) would inherit the world did not come to (him) or to his descendants through the law but through the righteousness of *faith*." Paul then draws a direct line between our faith and God's grace by writing, "For this reason the promise depends on *faith*, in order that it may rest on *grace*, so that it be guaranteed to all his descendants, not only to the adherents of the law but also to those who share the faith of Abraham."[7] And then a few lines later he says, "Therefore (Abraham's faith) was reckoned to him as righteousness."[8]

Well, that really settles it, doesn't it? The Faith card seems like a good card to play... but is it enough? Suddenly you remember James, presumably

---

7. Rom. 4:16.
8. Rom. 4:22.

the brother of Jesus, saying, "So faith by itself, if it has no works, is dead."[9] You want to play the Faith card, but then a thought creeps into your head, "Do I have *enough* Faith?" Is faith all that God really asks of us?

While you are pondering that question, you see the Belief card peering over the top of the Faith card. Aha! Maybe, you think, you can support your potential lack of faith with a few strong beliefs. Paul seems to agree that believing is important. He talks about the God that Abraham *believed* in. He noted that Abraham *believed* he would become "the father of many nations."[10] Now you are at the point where you believe you have it all figured out. Just to play it safe, you decide to play the Good Works card, the Faith card, *and* the Belief card. All you can do is hope that when Jesus sees you playing those cards, he will play the Grace card in response.

So, you lay the cards on the table, feeling pretty good about yourself... but then you notice something you didn't expect. You realize that the entire time you have been holding your cards, moving them around in your hand, considering which ones to play, *Jesus has already played the Grace card.*

GRACE IN THE GRADE BOOK

I'm not a schoolteacher, and I haven't had a child in school for a couple of decades, so I'm not well-informed about all the different ways students are graded. However, I did teach a few college courses 20–25 years ago, and I remember how difficult it was to be fair in my grading. I used the traditional system where students receive a letter grade—A to F—based on their average scores from 100 to 0. I didn't want to be too easy or too tough; I just wanted to be fair. Most of the time I used the "your grade is what you made" system. However, if I thought my exam was too difficult, I would grade on the curve or a sliding scale. Students get excited hearing they are being graded on a curve because it usually means their scores will move up a notch or two, based on what everyone else does. The downside of grading on a curve is that the students who score very high are often harassed for "throwing off the curve," so maybe it's best to keep that information private. That ambitious and studious "curve-buster" in the first row who made a 99 on the exam will likely end up eating alone in the cafeteria.

Grading was the most difficult part of being a teacher. This was especially true when I taught college courses in prison. Most of those guys

---

9. Jam. 2:17.
10. Rom. 4:17.

Grace

were well-behaved, respectful, and motivated to learn, so I didn't want to jeopardize my safety by giving an unfair exam. You don't want to be in lockdown with an inmate who just received an "F" on his research paper.

With all this grading in mind, let's get theological. According to Jesus, God is our teacher. In John 6:45, Jesus says, "It is written in the prophets, 'And they shall all be *taught* by God.' Everyone who has heard and learned from the Father comes to me." Okay, I'll bite. If God is our teacher, then how does God grade us, and what is God grading us for? Does God grade our belief systems, moral actions, and/or our intentions? I'm sure you've heard the old saying, "The road to hell is paved with good intentions," but is that true? Shouldn't our good intentions bump up our grade a notch or two?

How does God grade us? If I were God, I think I would consider three possible grading systems: The first possibility is "the Grade that you Made System." This is a very straightforward approach. All God must do is grade us based on whether our belief systems, moral actions, or intentions are passable or not. Easy-peasy. That shouldn't be a problem for God. God just whips out the ole divine calculator and tallies up our marks. I don't know about you, but I hope this is *not* the way God grades us. I'm with the psalmist on this, who writes, "If you, O Lord, should *mark* iniquities, Lord, who could stand?"[11] If God is grading our belief systems, moral actions, and intentions, most of us are probably heading for a big fat F.

Thankfully, most theologians do not believe God's grading system is a simple "the grade that you made" approach, or we would all be repeating the religious equivalent of First Grade. Very few, if any, would ever graduate. We hope that God's grading system shows a little more *grace* that that, which brings us to a second possible way God grades us: On the curve or with a sliding scale. This is probably what most folks believe. We are never going to ace God's exams, especially the final exam, on our own merit, so we hope that God gives us a big enough boost to move from fail to pass. Most of us are probably right on the cusp between failing and passing. There are likely a few authentic "saints" in our midst (who make an A on their religious report cards), and obviously there are a handful of horrible sinners (who receive an F on their report card), yet both of those groups are tiny.

Most of us fall somewhere between in terms of our belief systems, moral actions, and intentions, so we need a little help. This is why our

---

11. Ps. 130:3.

theology is infused with grace-sounding words such as God's steadfast love, forgiveness, mercy, redemption, and salvation. These words imply that, at the very least, God gives our grades a "grace bump." Psalm 130, which begins with the words of a failing student— "out of the depths I cry to you, O Lord"—concludes with the picture of a God who "will redeem Israel from all its iniquities." Notice that the psalmist doesn't say *some* of Israel's iniquities. He says *all* of Israel's iniquities. Perhaps we have stumbled upon a third possible way God grades our belief systems, moral actions, and intentions. More than a "grace bump," God gives us a "grace ace." God's grace takes us all the way to the top.

We are all valedictorians according to God's Grace Ace System of Grading. According to this theory, God gives everyone who shows up and takes the test an A+. We have good reason to think this is God's grading system because Jesus is the one who brought us the Grace Ace System of Grading. In John's gospel, he uses language like "anyone who comes to me I will never drive away," and "Whoever believes has *eternal life*."[12] Receiving eternal life is like receiving a perfect score on an exam, even if we haven't earned it. After all, there's no way to *earn* eternal life. It must be gifted to us.

This is hard for us to comprehend. We can't imagine a teacher telling her students, "Just show up to class and you'll get an A+," although some teachers *do* give extra credit for good or perfect attendance. Still, grace (on any level or to any degree) is a difficult concept to grasp. It suggests God's grading system is not "fair" in the way we understand fairness. The God of the Bible, the God of Jesus, seems to go beyond fairness.

As I reflect on God as a Teacher, and how God might grade our belief systems, moral actions, and intentions, I have a few other thoughts to share, such as:

Maybe God factors in "level of difficulty" in the divine grading system, just as the Olympic judges, at some of the events, give extra points to athletes based on the level of difficulty of their routines. Maybe the more difficult our lives are, the more grace we get on our final exams. Just a thought.

Maybe God has given us an "Open-Book" exam. I'm talking about the Bible, of course, but also God's creation or nature. All the answers to the "final exam" are right in front of us. We might even call the Bible and nature "cheat sheets."

Maybe there are no right or wrong answers to God's exams. God doesn't give us multiple-choice or true/false questions that seek correct or

---

12. Jn. 6:37, 47.

incorrect answers. Instead, maybe God grades us as if our lives are like creative essays or poetry. There are no wrong answers in creative essays and poetry. At best, maybe we're graded on "style points."

There is so much to think about in terms of God's possible grading system. For example, in my research for this essay, I found the following random quote from an evangelical pastor: "God doesn't grade on a curve; God grades on the cross." I guess that means Jesus made a perfect score and we get to copy his paper. We can go in a lot of provocative directions with this whole divine grading system thing, but my final thought is this: Maybe God initially grades us by marking down all our iniquities as the writer of Psalm 130 suggests, but then after tallying them up and seeing such a huge number, God looks at Jesus, his Teacher's Aide, gives a nod, and Jesus hits the "all clear" button on the calculator, which is a perfect way to describe Christianity Lite.

15

The Heavy Issue of Identity

CHRISTIANITY LITE NEEDS TO take a pragmatic approach to religion and society. In this book, I have described in creative and sometimes light-hearted ways how this Lite flavor of faith is undergirded by various principles. I have applied these principles to various Christian theological conversations. In many of these essays, I have relied on contemporary analogies. The reader may find that I used far too many sports analogies (unless the reader happens to be a sports fan). I might have left social justice warrior-types feeling slighted, although those on the right may walk away slightly more offended. My rationale for keeping my distance from too many "heavy" issues is that I feel the need to do the philosophical work first so that when we come to any hard-won conclusions on social issues, we can do so without stomping on people in a heavy-footed manner. In my opinion, Christianity Lite offers us an opportunity to speak *with* one another rather than *at* one another. It compels us to lay down our verbal weaponry and find a pragmatic, if not middle ground on issues that currently divide in irredeemable ways.[1]

Speaking of divisive issues, I have decided to throw my hat into the ring in the ongoing debate about identity. Long before identity politics became a thing, yet more so since it became a thing, human beings have been aware of their identity markers, such as ethnicity, national origin,

---

1. By using the phrase "middle ground," I do not believe that we literally need to find the *median* in our disagreements. I do not believe there are always or even often viewpoints that are opposite and equal in terms of correctness. Surely, there is a right and wrong perspective in our social debates. Just as important, however, is the notion that there is a right and wrong way to engage in debates. Sometimes, gradualism is required, while at other times a firm, unbending position is appropriate. Sometimes, a light-hearted approach is preferable to a heavy-handed screech, and sometimes we are compelled to scream loudly.

gender, sexual orientation, socioeconomic status, age, religion, and mental, emotional, or physical abilities and disabilities. Historically, our fears and prejudices about crossing socially acceptable boundaries of identity markers included outlawing "mixed race breeding," as if the results would be as horrifying as an elephant mating with a hippopotamus, and promoting eugenics, which was heralded to be able to produce a superior race. These days we have rejected both extreme positions, and yet we continue to be preoccupied with identity markers.

We are obsessed with our DNA results because we want to know who we are, sometimes completely ignoring the fact that nurture (environment) is just as important, if not more so, than nature (genetics) in the way we present ourselves to society. John Locke's *tabula rasa*, or blank slate, is not the only tablet on which our lives are written. As our brains develop and self-awareness takes root, we become exposed to different experiences and learn behaviors that quickly become quasi-deterministic characteristics in the makeup of our personhood. We are extremely complex and complicated beings, and not just because men are from Mars and women are from Venus.[2]

Because of our obsession with identity, we live in an era when our identity markers are markedly more visual and visceral by design. Take the ubiquitous *flags*, for example. I don't recall as many flags waving from front yard flagpoles or the tail end of pickup trucks in all my born days as I do today. In my immediate area alone, I have spotted the following flags fluttering in the firmament: American, Texan, Mexican, and the rest of the "Six Flags over Texas" collection of flags. Curiously, I see the occasional Ukrainian, Israeli, or Scottish flag—the latter reflecting my genetic roots. I see a surprising number of Trump (MAGA), Don't Tread on Me, Come and Take it, and Confederate flags, as well as Rainbow, Black Lives Matter, and Earth flags competing for the same neighborhood's sovereignty. There are also flags representing one's favorite university or high school, and even the Christian flag. Flags might be the hip thing these days, but they are not our only visible expressions of identification. There are tee shirts, tattoos, bumper stickers, political campaign signs, and even denominational or church signs with their stylish logos glowing in the dark.

In the context of this identity warfare, if there is one place, one institution, one haven from all identification conflict, it should be Christ's church.

---

2. Gray, *Men Are from Mars*. We all come from stardust, so who knows?

That statement requires an explanation that will likely ruffle everyone's feathers. So, here goes.

The Irish postmodern philosopher/theologian, Peter Rollins, is the intellectual muse for the Emergent Church, a postmodern expression of Christianity popular in the last quarter of a century. Rollins is what a lay person might call "out there." He is a non-academic, non-clergyperson known for a "religion-less" interpretation of Christianity that he calls "pyro-theology"—think "deconstruction with a match."[3] Or rather a torch. He writes in the traditions of apophatic, death of God, and existential theology. He's not your average bear. Take my word for it: his works don't preach in our evangelical-leaning culture.

In his interpretation and application of the identity-laden passage found in Galatians 3:26–28, Rollins relies on "neither/nor" language rather than "both/and" or "either/or."[4] The following is the Common English Bible's version of this passage: "You are all God's children through faith in Christ Jesus. All of you who were baptized into Christ have clothed yourselves with Christ. There is neither Jew nor Greek; there is neither slave nor free; nor is there male and female, for you are all one in Christ Jesus."

In this passage, Paul lists three examples of binary identity markers that were relevant in his day: ethnicity/religion (Jew or Greek), political (slave or free), and gender (male or female). The obvious takeaway from this passage is that Paul is downplaying the significance of these binary oppositional identity markers. Remember, Paul is the same guy who led a movement to remove the requirement (and importance) of the most visible identity marker one could possibly imagine in that place and time: circumcision. This applied only to males, of course, but it's not a stretch to assume that the women were identified through the male members of her family. If she was hanging onto a man's arm, she had the same status as he did.

Paul, a Jewish Pharisee of the pro-circumcision crowd in his former life, effectively said, "No, put down the knives. We are not interested in your identity markers. Depend only on Christ for comfort and cover." Perhaps because identity is so "fluid," to borrow a word that is common in today's identity politics, Christians continue to fly real or metaphorical flags of identification, depending upon where they can find comfort and cover. And by "cover" I mean groups that keep people from being doomed to Lone Ranger status. Everyone dabbles in identity politics, even within

---

3. Rollins, "Pyrotheology."
4. Rollins, *Insurrection*, 164–171.

the confines of the Christian faith. The fight is real and robust. It is almost all-consuming in the sense that it takes up most of the oxygen in the room these days.

To dissect this further, I will rely on a couple of common identity markers, "conservative" and "liberal," as I generalize and over-simplify their positions for the sake of expediency. Obviously, there are always exceptions to the rule, outliers, and in-house rebels.

First, the conservatives, who historically have tended to utilize "either/or" language in terms of race or ethnicity, arguing that we are either this or that, Jew or gentile, black or white or brown. Anything outside of historically defined ethnic markers is confusing, frowned upon, or even condemned. While many conservatives have moved beyond strict binary thinking in terms of race and ethnicity, in terms of gender expression, we are either male or female. Anything "in between" is confusing, frowned upon, or outright condemned. Due to their either/or worldview, conservatives are uncomfortable with in-between or fluid categories such as transgender, gender neutral, non-binary, etc.

In terms of sexual orientation, their either/or stance has led them to proclaim a "this, but *not* that" ethic. Fortunately, as is true with many other issues, the sheer passage of time and the constant drumbeat of awareness of minority sexual orientations within most families or circles of friends has led many conservatives to a softer version of "this, and hopefully not that." In terms of gender expression, conservatives are not yet budging very much, but in terms of sexual orientation, they are allowing the goal posts to be moved ever so slowly. If I may use another sports analogy, conservatives are playing *defense*. And lest you think this means they will inevitably lose the game, recall what many a football aficionado has claimed over the years: "Defense wins championships."[5]

And then there are the liberals. Whereas conservatives tend to play defense in terms of identity politics, liberals are naturally bent toward playing offense. They tend to push the envelope, expand boundaries, muddy the waters, and erase the clear and distinct lines of past social norms. Whereas both conservatives and liberals are trying to push an "agenda," one could make the case that liberals are engaged in pushing their agenda more aggressively. Liberals are more *on* offense; thus, they are more *offensive* in the

---

5. This phrase is often credited to Bear Bryant, who led the Alabama Crimson Tide to six championships during his tenure with the team. "Defense wins championships," Wikipedia, http://en.m.wikipedia.org.

sense that their agenda often angers and upsets their opponents (which doesn't necessarily mean they are wrong). Conservatives do this as well, but in a way that is already historically acknowledged. Certainly, conservative identity politics hurts, angers, and upsets their opponents, but their opponents have already seen that movie. There is an emotional buffer that is already established here.

In contrast to the conservative "either/or" approach, liberals take a "both/and" approach. This "both/and" approach has created, for the sake of simplicity, an alphabet of options in terms of both gender identity and sexual preference, often communicated as "LGBTQIA+".[6]

So, what does all this mean for the church? My biggest problem with identity politics playing out so frequently in congregational life is that I believe both ideological approaches to identity issues result in heavy-handed *exclusivism*. They are not exclusive to the same degree, of course. The liberal approach is closer to a more palatable Christian ethic, yet the results are similar. Generally speaking (because remember, I am over-simplifying and generalizing), ultra-conservatives *overtly and directly* exclude those who do not fit into their either/or worldview, while liberals *covertly and indirectly* exclude those who do not accept their both/and approach to identity issues. So-called "moderates" merely occupy the center lanes of these two highways. A moderate might win the "congeniality" trophy at the Ethics Awards ceremony, but they are still on the same highway, although driving more cautiously and willing to make an occasional U-turn.

It is my view that the liberal approach is on the right side of history. A "both/and" approach to identity politics is a more generous and ethical approach. It is clearly the result of planting one's flag on moral high ground. However, *in the context of congregational life*, wearing the identity garb of any group outside of our baptized community puts us on the wrong path. Let the feather ruffling begin.

I realize that I am firmly planted, rooted, and continue to sprout in the infamous "male, pale, stale, and straight" community. Anything I say about this, or any other topic, could be construed as mansplaining by default. No one has any obligation whatsoever to consider my words or even read them. Nevertheless, human discourse requires us to submit our perspective, no matter how tainted it might be from the ravages of human

---

6. Personally, although not an official card-carrying member of these communities (unless they find a letter representing "male, pale, stale, and straight allies"), I prefer a more poetic and less prosaic term such as "rainbow community" to be used as an umbrella designation for minority gender expressions and sexual preferences.

shortsightedness, to create an environment where honest people can respond and further the conversation in beneficial ways. I say all this in the context of congregations and denominations siphoning off members at an alarming rate, primarily because of their persistent emphasis on identity issues. The results have been catastrophic to most denominations.

Conservative evangelical groups, playing defense, have effectively excluded sexual and gender minorities from even considering membership in their congregations. For the most part, they have moved past their history of racial segregation, although racism continues to be deeply embedded in all American Christianity. Conservatives are losing *potential* members rather than *active* members. Their membership data doesn't necessarily reflect the loss of potential members. When they do lose active members because of identity issues, young people are the ones leaving in droves because they have become uncomfortable with the undisguised and unapologetic homophobia, transphobia, and sexism in their church homes.[7]

Liberal mainline groups, on the other hand, are playing offense. Due to this stance, they are experiencing the loss of already active members, many of whom have spent their entire lives in their home congregations. They often cite their denomination's liberal and open stance toward sexual and gender minorities as proof that these denominations are no longer representative of them. The progressive and evolving stances of these denominations have left them behind theologically and socially. Conservative members are not being overtly excluded—they are not being asked or compelled to leave—but they no longer feel comfortable or even welcomed in their mainline congregations. Because of this phenomenon, the mainline church is losing members and congregations, especially in small towns and rural areas.

Again, the stance of the mainline denominations is surely on the right side of history. There is a right and wrong approach to identity issues. The wrong approach is exclusive, and the right approach is inclusive. And yet both sides are suffering numerically. There are people from both sides of the ideological spectrum that feel alienated from their potential or actual congregations or denominations. Both sides of this debate are losing either potential or active members.

This compels me to ask a question: Should identity politics, even from an inclusive perspective, be part of the mission of the Church? Obviously, it behooves us to pursue fairness, equality, and justice in terms of race,

---

7. Kinnaman, *UnChristian*, 91–119.

ethnicity, gender, sexuality, and all the other identity markers that currently represent the human species. People should use their platforms—from social media to bullhorns to political activism—as much as they can to support their positions. And yet, if we are talking about identity within the context of the church, perhaps we need to recapture the spirit of the early Christian movement, *a movement that was trying to bring people together from various backgrounds.*

The Apostle Paul, in his letter to the Galatians uses the analogy of "clothing." He writes, "All of you who were baptized into Christ have clothed yourselves with Christ," and then he offers his "neither/nor" list of possible Christ-followers, such as Jews, Greeks, slaves, the politically free, males and females. He knows better than anyone that there are some very real disagreements and distinctions among these variously clothed members of Christ's body. He knows there are always oppressors and oppressed, justice-oriented folks and prejudiced people, people on the right side of history and those who haven't yet "caught up." He knows that everyone has a metaphorical flag or two. Everyone has identity markers that provide comfort and cover to those who fall into the same demographics. And yet, Paul knows that the only way to build a whole body out of a fractured population is to convince them to wear the same clothing, metaphorically speaking. Christianity is an anti-fashion movement, a school uniform religion, where no one wears anything that would make them stand out and be unique or better (or worse), a safe space where hierarchies of identities are dismantled for the sake of cohesion and community.

Because the stakes of identity politics are so high, all of us will continue to feel compelled to fly our flags even higher so that people will know exactly where we "stand." I *under*stand. As a white, straight, cisgender male, the ground I stand on has flown more flags over its head than Texas. I couldn't give up my stake even if I tried. And yet, in the church—in Christ's church—we should recognize everyone as an equal. We should lay down our flags and pick up the moniker of "God's children," spiritual descendants of Abraham (Gal. 3:29). At least while we are spreading the message of unconditional love, we should lay down the conditional flags. We should stop the bleeding and the demise of Christ's family. They say, "Blood is thicker than water," but the truest confession of the church, more eloquent than all the creeds, is that the waters of baptism are thicker than the blood of humanity.

Bibliography

Ahern, Cecelia. *Love, Rosie*. New York: Grand Central, 2006.
Amoskala. "The Melting Pot vs. the Salad Bowl." *Black and Green Atlantic* (2020).
Aristotle. *Nicomachean Ethics*. University of Chicago Press, 2012.
Barad, Judith, with Ed Robertson. *The Ethics of Star Trek*. New York: HarperCollins, 2000.
Borg, Marcus. *Meeting Jesus Again for the First Time: The Historical Jesus and the Heart of Contemporary Faith*. San Francisco: HarperSanFrancisco, 1994.
Brueggemann, Walter. *Spirituality of the Psalms (Facets)*. Minneapolis: Fortress, 2001.
Carder, Kenneth L. "A Wesleyan Understanding of Grace." ResourceUMC. http://www.resourceumc.org.
The Clash. "Should I Stay or Should I Go?" Track 3 on Combat Rock. CBS Records, 1982.
Crossan, John Dominic. *Jesus: A Revolutionary Biography: A Startling Account of What We Can Know About the Life of Jesus*. San Francisco: HarperSanFrancisco, 1994.
Durant, Will. *The Story of Philosophy*. New York: Simon & Schuster, 1926.
Flanders, Henry Jackson, Jr., Robert Wilson Crapps, and David Anthony Smith. *People of the Covenant: An Introduction to the Hebrew Bible*. Oxford University Press, 1988.
"Four Levels of Volunteering." *Influence Magazine* (2017). https://influencemagazine.com/Practice/Four-Levels-of-Volunteering.
Gardner, Howard. *Frames of Mind: The Theory of Multiple Intelligences*. New York: Basic, 1983.
Garn, Talmage. "Needle Me This: Vinyl's Spinning Story." http://www.bobfmutah.com.
Gladwell, Malcolm. *Revenge of the Tipping Point: Overstories, Superspreaders, and the Rise of Social Engineering*. New York: Hachette, 2024.
Gray, John. *Men Are from Mars, Women Are from Venus: A Practical Guide for Improving Communication and Getting What You Want in Your Relationships*. New York: HarperCollins, 1992.
Gulley, Philip, and James Mulholland. *If Grace Is True: Why God Will Save Every Person*. San Francisco: HarperOne, 2010.
Heyl, Julia Childs. "The Flynn Effect: What's Behind Rising IQ Scores?" *Verywellmind* (2024). http://www.verywellmind.com. .
Jones, Jeffrey M. "U.S. Church Membership Falls below Majority for First Time." *Gallup News* (2021). https://news.gallup.com.
Joyce, James. *Finnegans Wake*. London: Faber and Faber, 1939.
Kinnaman, David and Gabe Lyons. *UnChristian: What a New Generation Really Thinks about Christianity . . . and Why It Matters*. Ada, Michigan: Baker, 2007.

Bibliography

Klawans, Justin. "A Disproven Medical Theory Could be Guiding RFK Jr.'s Health Policy." *The Week.* http://www.theweek.com.

Kondo, Marie. *The Life-Changing Magic of Tidying Up: The Japanese Art of Decluttering and Organizing.* Emeryville, California: Ten Speed, 2014.

Lennon, John. "Imagine." Track 1 on *Imagine.* Produced by John Lennon and Yoko Ono. Apple, 1971.

Marchese, David. "How to Live a Happy Life, From a Leading Atheist." *The New York Times,* August 27, 2023. http://www.nytimes.com.

"Marie Kondo and the Life-Changing Magic of Japanese Soft Power." *The New York Times,* January 18, 2019. http://www.nytimes.com.

Nelson, Paul. "Jackson Browne: The Rolling Stone Interview." *Rolling Stone* (1980). http://www.rollingstone.com.

"Nothing off Limits in Scrum at the Bottom of NFL Pileup." *NFL.com* (2010). http://www.nfl.com.

Osmanski, Stephanie. "This Might Be the Most Annoying Corporate Jargon Phrase Ever?" *MSN* (2024). https://www.msn.com.

Plantinga, Alvin. *God, Freedom, and Evil.* Grand Rapids: Eerdmans, 1977.

Putnam, Robert. *Bowling Alone: The Collapse and Revival of American Community.* New York: Simon & Schuster, 2001.

Rohr, Richard. *Falling Upward: A Spirituality for the Two Halves of Life.* San Francisco: Jossey-Bass, 2011.

Rollins, Peter. *Insurrection: To Believe is Human, To Doubt, Divine.* Brentwood, Tennessee: Howard, 2011.

———. "Pyrotheology: An Introduction." *Peterrollins.com.* http://www.peterrollins.com.

Rushnell, Squire. *When God Winks: How the Power of Coincidence Guides Your Life.* Brentwood, Tennessee: Howard, 2002.

Shakespeare, William. *The Tempest.* 1611.

Smith, Jeremy. "Hacking Christianity: What Happens When We Apply a Computer Coding Debate to Christian Doctrine." *Hacking Christianity* (2021). https://hackingchristianity.net.

Snider, Phil, ed. *The Hyphenateds: How Emergence Christianity is Re-Traditioning Mainline Practices.* St. Louis: Chalice, 2011.

Tennyson, Alfred Lord. "In Memoriam A.H.H." 1850.

Wikipedia. "Leaving the World a Better Place." Wikimedia Foundation, last updated Aug 11, 2025. https://en.wikipedia.org/wiki/Leaving_the_world_a_better_place.

———. "Popeye." Wikimedia Foundation, last updated Aug 25, 2025. https://en.wikipedia.org/wiki/Popeye.

Wren, Jon. "Religion." *Christian Standard* (2020). http://christianstandard.com.

Zimet, Abby. "Finding A Way: Good Trouble Lives On." *Common Dreams* (2025). https://www.commondreams.org.